W9-DFP-070

An Army of Davids

Herman Cain & Rich Lowrie

Velocity • MASCOT

Requests for permission to make copies of any part of the work should be submitted online to info@mascotbooks.com or mailed to:

Velocity • Mascot
560 Herndon Parkway #120
Herndon, VA 20170.

ISBN-10: 1-620860-30-9
ISBN-13: 978-1-620860-30-4
CPSIA Code: PRR0512B

Cover artwork by Joshua Taggert

Printed in the United States

www.mascotbooks.com
www.velocity-books.com

To Gloria, Melanie, and Vincent, Celena, Preston, Ryan, and Jason. Family first!

—Herman Cain

To my daughters Rachel and Ryann, I do this because I want to give you a country that has at least as much opportunity as the one my parents gave to me.

—Rich Lowrie

"I believe there are more instances of the abridgment of the freedom of the people by gradual and silent encroachments of those in power, than by violent and sudden usurpations."

—James Madison

Acknowledgements

Rich Lowrie and I have many people to thank for their help in making this book possible. If we thanked them all, we'd have another book, but a few we want to single out regardless.

We start with Friends of Herman Cain Economic Policy Advisory Committee members: Chuck Kadlec, Brian Domitrovic, Paul Hoffmeister, Louis Woodhill, and David Burton. I will put this team up against any. My energy advisers are too numerous to list but deserve thanks.

Next, Gary Robbins for scoring and technical support with tax tables, Dan Calabrese for his exceptional editing work, and Clark Barrow for research assistance.

Things happen for a reason, so we also want to thank the Club for Growth, which is where Rich and I met. At their conference, we also met Rich Vedder, who later introduced Rich to Lew Uhler, who eventually introduced Rich to Mark Block, who later became my campaign manager and gave Rich the opportunity to work with my campaign.

We are grateful to Americans for Prosperity for giving Rich, Mark, and me our own opportunities to pursue pro-growth reform, in some cases working together.

Without Rich's business partner, Wayne Carney, holding down the fort with the assistance of Ronda and Trisha, this book would not be possible.

The influence over many years of Stephen Moore and Larry Kudlow can be found throughout the book. Thanks to the late Jack Kemp and Jude Wanniski for their foresight, insight, and persistence on behalf of a better country.

Finally, special thanks to Bob Mundell and Arthur Laffer for showing the way forward, not just for us, but for the world. We followed them, and we hope others will join us.

Table of Contents

Introduction

When it comes to our U.S. tax code, we are either stuck on stupid or just plain stupid.

If we were ignorant of the fact that our tax code is one of the most archaic, ineffective and inefficient systems on the planet, we could say that we just don't know any better. But we do know better! And since 1913, we have allowed the tax code monster to consume our time, our money, our business decisions, our national creativity, our lives, our nation – and even our common sense.

Granted, some people in high places would like to keep the current tax system in place because it lets them manipulate, misuse and abuse it to influence people's behavior. They use it to gain selfish tax favors for their own interests, and to eliminate special tax treatments for other folk. It's a loopholes merry-go-round.

But those of us in low places – those of us who simply have a job or are pursuing a career, or are running a business, or trying to take care of our families –are sick and tired of being sick and tired of the current tax code.

We need a national day of "scream" to protest the insanity of the tax code and the inability – or lack of desire – of Washington to fix the problem. That's why "We the People" will have to fix it by becoming an "Army of Davids" – an army ready to take on the Philistine Goliath with nothing in our bags but five smooth stones.

Big government Goliath is going down! We want our power back!

The people are not stupid. They don't always have the information they should have, because the people who are supposed to give it to them don't do that. That's why not all of the people understand the solutions that are necessary. Yet.

When the people understand it, they will demand it. They will understand that we must replace the tax code. Tinkering around the edges has never worked, and will never work.

Throw it out and start all over.

The **9-9-9** Economic Growth and Jobs Plan is a new start to growing our economy. It will unleash businesses to grow using their entrepreneurial spirit and determination, and provide a job or career for everyone who wants to succeed in the old-fashioned, never-go-out-of-style, United States of America way.

Work for it!

That's what our parents did. We did it, too. And that's what we need to give our grandchildren: an opportunity to prosper under the **9-9-9** tax plan.

It treats all taxpayers the same, and all businesses the same. It treats U.S.-made goods and services like goods from most foreign countries, and eliminates the loopholes merry-go-round. To me, that's fair. To listen to people in political circles, you'd think I'm the only one who sees it that way. But that's not the truth.

Washington's collective inability to really fix a problem is not new. But an "Army of Davids," a people's movement, will bring the heat to make Washington see the light. That light is called **9-9-9**.

When you finish reading this book, you will be informed, intellectually involved and inspired. You will be a "David" joining thousands of other Davids to get the giant's foot off our neck.

I'm Herman Cain. We are not stupid.

9-9-9

An Army of Davids

Chapter 1

Tinkering Won't Work

> *When you want to help people, you tell them the truth. When you want to help yourself, you tell them what they want to hear.*
>
> *—Thomas Sowell*

Defeating Obama Is the Key to a Jobs Recovery

President Obama is not very good at economic policy. But he is very clever about making you think he is—unless you pay very close attention.Consider: Unemployment remains well above 8 percent, which is considerably higher than the day Obama took office. It has remained above 8 percent longer than any period since the Depression. Real unemployment, which includes the underemployed and those who have given up looking, is nearly 15 percent. And yet Obama goes around talking about the private-sector job growth we've been having. If that's true, why is unemployment still so high?

Because Obama only tells you the part of the story that makes him look good.

In his 2012 State of the Union address, Obama spoke glowingly about the recent job creation. He said: "In the last twenty-two months, businesses have created more than three million jobs. Last year, they created the most jobs since 2005."

Sounds pretty good. But I wondered, why twenty-two months? Being a mathematician, I decided to take a closer look.

When I did so, the first thing I remembered was that the best way to measure a recovery is from the prior peak, not the bottom of the recession. In other words: Did we regain what we lost, and how long did it take? To measure gains from the beginning of the recovery ignores the damage done by the recession! For example, let's say we had one hundred jobs and lost fifty in a recession, only to regain twenty-five in the recovery. The two opposing ways to look at it are technically both true:

1. We are still down twenty-five jobs from the prior peak.
2. Jobs are up 50 percent in the recovery! Yay!

If we measure from the prior peak, this is by far the worst recovery since the Great Depression. It is the worst in terms of how far below the peak we still are and how long it is taking to climb back. In terms of job creation, Team Obama is further behind the previous worst recovery than the previous worst recovery is from the best recovery. To have that far to go just to catch up and tie for last place, and to be bragging about it, is the equivalent of getting a ribbon for ninth place and thinking you've won something.

To be sure, this was a sharp recession. But that is not a defense of Obama's weak recovery. There is a well-established pattern that the sharper the recession, the sharper the recovery. Think of how a rubber band snaps back. So the sharpness of the recession is not an excuse for the weakness of the recovery. It is a further indictment of it. In fact, this is the only scenario on record that couples a sharp recession with an anemic recovery.

That's why Obama only shows you the picture from the time the recovery started. It's only without the context of what happened during the recession that he can persuade you this is a good performance.

But for fun, let's grant the premise that it is not misleading to measure the recovery from the bottom of the recession (ignoring all the damage done during the recession) rather than from the prior peak. Comparing apples to apples, the other recessions that were similarly sharp occurred in 1953, 1957, 1973–1974, and 1981–1982. Figure 1-1 shows what it looks like if you compare only the recoveries that followed these past sharp recessions.

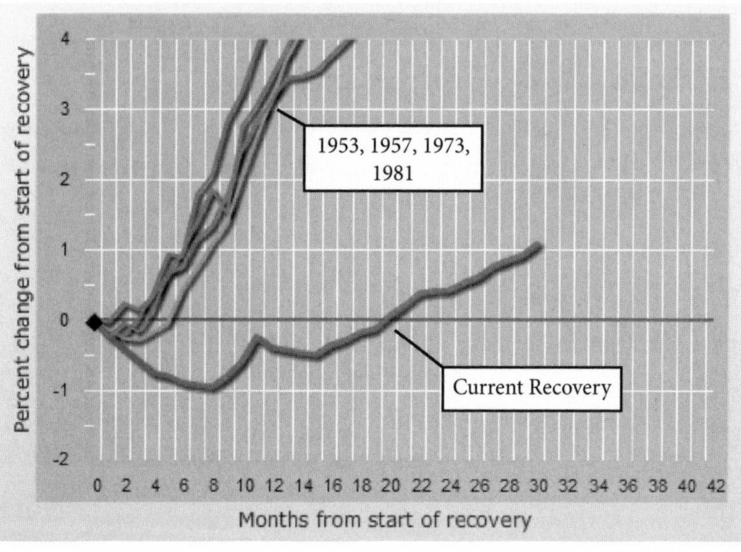

Figure 1-1. U.S. employment recoveries after sharp recessions. (Federal Reserve Bank of Minneapolis; updated January 6, 2012)

We are obviously far behind where we should be. In fact, we are eating the dust of all prior recoveries.

Figure 1-2 shows what the recovery looks like using the more acceptable method of measuring from the prior peak.

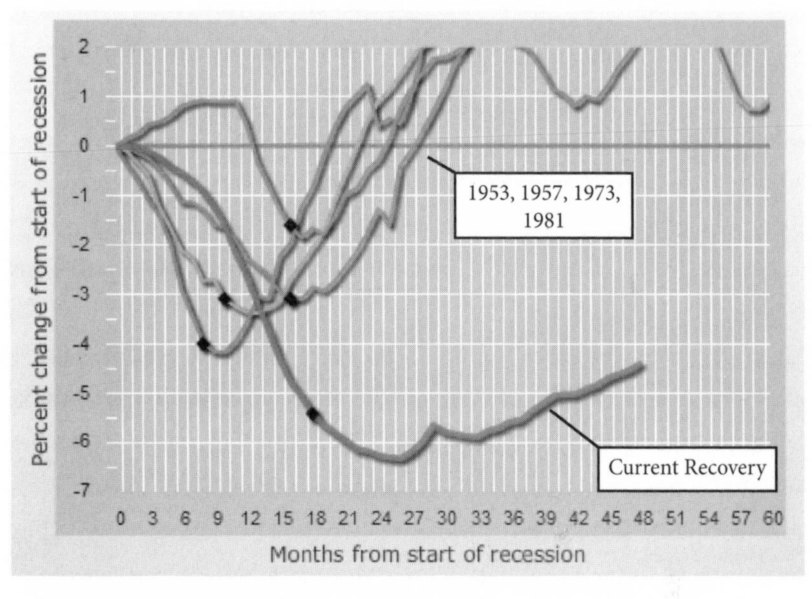

Figure 1-2. U.S. employment recoveries after sharp recessions. (Federal Reserve Bank of Minneapolis; updated January 6, 2012)

What is noteworthy on this chart is that even after the start of the recovery (marked by the black diamond), we still continued to lose jobs. This is the only recovery from a sharp recession that has done that. In all past recoveries following sharp recessions, job growth picked up almost immediately, and there was no looking back. In this so-called recovery, we continued to steadily shed jobs for nine months after the official recovery started. So even the biased metric of measuring only the recovery doesn't explain Obama's twenty-two months.

As a math major and a problem solver, I am determined to get the answer.

Are you ready for something really hilarious? Why did Obama mention "the last twenty-two months" in his 2012 State of the Union address? It is simply the lowest point of the current recovery line in the employment graph shown in Figure 1-2 (which corresponds with month 26 on the chart). It is the date that makes him look the best in this otherwise lousy jobs environment. Other than that, it does not correspond to anything, such as his election, his inauguration, the "stimulus," Obamacare, or anything for which credit can deservingly be claimed by Obama.

Here is the irony: count backward twenty-two months from the December data used in the president's 2012 address. That brings us to February 2010. What was the major news story then? The Scott Brown Senate victory in Massachusetts! The sixtieth vote was taken away from Czar Obama. What says "repudiation" more than when Massachusetts, of all states, elects a Republican to Ted Kennedy's old seat to stop the force-feeding of the Obama agenda? This marked the turning point where we could say the worst was over and the onslaught from the left had been halted. It proved to be the bellwether of the 2010 congressional landslide. It was an event that defined the end of the Obama agenda.

Any coincidence that hiring picked up after this? I think not. As a successful businessman, I can say firsthand that an environment based on the premise that the beatings will continue until morale improves is not the most conducive to job creation. Basically, there is nothing for which Obama can claim credit during these twenty-two months. In fact, just the opposite. His agenda was stopped. He should credit the Tea Party the next time he quotes any job growth that occurred after his agenda was repudiated. Expect job growth to continue as we approach the elections—if it looks as if he will be defeated. The more businesses anticipate a return to pro-growth policies, the more likely they are to hire today.

Stopping his agenda was the key to some job growth. Replacing him is the key to robust job growth.

Repeal Obamacare or All Bets Are Off

There is no point talking about growth, jobs, or opportunity if Obamacare remains intact. It is economically devastating to our future. As soon as the government controls your health care, it controls you. It will have the justification to tell you what to eat, what to do, and how to live your life. This means unprecedented power over you and virtually every aspect of your life. Imagine the power bureaucrats will wield over every business, too. Businesses will have to curry favor with bureaucrats or risk having their products labeled "bad for you."

If you think lobbying for tax breaks is bad, just wait until business survival depends on it. As we should know by now, progressives will use any means to grab power and take away your liberty, and Obamacare is the mother of all vehicles for doing so. Talk about a Trojan horse! It is well-known that your happiness has an impact on your health. It won't be long before bureaucrats try to control even that.

Ultimately, a bureaucracy will determine who lives and who dies. Obamacare steals our freedom. For the sake of liberty, it must be repealed! Without liberty, is there really any point discussing growth and opportunity?

Aside from the constitutionality and morality issues (as if they aren't enough) government-run health care is bad economics. Rather than reduce costs, it will explode costs. A forced-through bill—which no one in Congress had time to read, the public didn't want, and that depended on parliamentary trickery to pass—claimed it would reduce costs, but it will actually increase them substantially and rob us of our freedom. It doesn't get any worse than that. The only way to get the economics this wrong is if the intent was not to provide health care but to rob us of liberty.

To get the picture clearly, look at the dishonest way the bill's sponsors sold it. In submitting cost estimates to the Congressional Budget Office, Obama counted the same $500 billion twice: both as

Medicaid savings and as money to pay for the bill. Obama's secretary of Health and Human Services, Kathleen Sebelius, admitted this in congressional testimony in March 2011—but those who had been paying attention were already well aware of the deceit. This wasn't the only example. In order to get the ten-year price tag of the law under $1 trillion—which they saw as politically important—the Obama administration delayed full implementation until 2014. That allowed them to count ten years' worth of revenues but only six years' worth of costs and thus claim that Obamacare reduced the deficit.

Since then, every new year has brought a new ten-year projection that adds a new year of cost, because we keep getting a year closer to implementation. The most recent ten-year cost projection was $1.7 trillion. What changed? Nothing. Obama knew this all along. He just had to hide the facts in order to get the bill past. As Nancy Pelosi said, we needed to pass it so we could find out what was in it. Well, guess what: we did!

How's that working out for ya?

Obamacare is a classic case of a "solution" that fails because it wasn't focused on the right problem—and that's one of the first principles I brought out of my business experience. You have to always work on the right problems. Working on the wrong problems only compounds them and doesn't solve anything.

To work on the right health-care problem, let's start with these two basic questions: Do we have a cost problem because we have an uninsured problem? Or do have an uninsured problem because we have a cost problem? If you believe that we have a cost problem because we have an uninsured problem, you favor an individual mandate. This is Obama and Romney. Romneycare is not a "state's right" or a "state's solution for a state's issues," as the governor alleges, but a fundamental misdiagnosis of the real problem. When technocrats make such mistakes, progressives always seize the opportunity to take power.

We have out-of-control costs because we do not have enough market forces in health care and have not had them for over fifty years. That's right. The government distorted the marketplace by granting a World War II–era tax preference for employer-provided health care that bypassed wage and price controls that were in effect at the time. It gave a deduction to employers without treating the noncash benefit to the employee as taxable compensation.

Essentially, this ushered in an era of overconsumption of tax-free health benefits. If you are going to tax the supply of a product and subsidize the consumption of that product, wouldn't you expect demand to outpace supply? When that happens, wouldn't you expect constant upward pressure on prices? Would the solution ever be to further restrict supply and increase demand? That's stupid!

This preferential treatment tilted the playing field in one direction, in favor of employer-provided coverage and away from individual policy ownership, let alone simply paying your own bills with your own money. It's like picking up one end of a pool table and having all the balls roll to the other end: every shot from that point forward will be distorted. The answer is not more distortion but a leveling of the playing field. Last I checked, World War II is over and we are no longer under wage and price controls (although, ironically, Obamacare is exactly a system of wage and price controls applied to health care), so the reason this policy was implemented no longer applies.

But it remains, and as a result, health insurance is the only form of insurance that you lose when you change jobs. Why don't you automatically lose your auto insurance every time you change jobs? Why not your homeowner's insurance, life insurance, long-term-care insurance, or any other individually owned policy?

People with perfectly fine coverage are forced to drop health coverage when they change jobs or are laid off. If a fully covered person gets sick but is then forced to drop coverage as a result of a job change, is it any wonder we have an uninsured problem? If you owned your own policy, this wouldn't happen. If you own a life insurance policy and later become uninsurable, you don't lose your policy by changing jobs. As long as you pay the premiums, your policy is yours.

Further, if we structured auto insurance the way we do health insurance, all of your gas and oil changes would be covered, and you would make a $20 co-pay each time you visited the gas station. There would be absolutely no reason to worry about gas prices. Auto insurance costs would skyrocket! It seems too ridiculous to discuss, but that is exactly how health insurance operates.

We clearly have an uninsured problem because we have a cost problem, and the cost problem is driven by government expenditures (direct expenditures plus tax expenditures) on health care. The president's own Council of Economic Advisers said in June 2009, before passage of Obamacare, "There is well documented evidence that individuals respond to lower cost-sharing by using more care, as well as more expensive care, when they do not face the full price of their decisions at the point of utilization." Imagine what individuals do when the government makes health care "free."

Please tell the Obama administration there is no free lunch.

Consumers should be price- and value-conscious in purchasing health care, and they should be rewarded for thrifty decisions just as they are in purchasing every other good or service. Providers, conversely, get no reward for providing exceptional value, but they should.

People respond to incentives. When the price of something increases, they have an incentive to consume less while suppliers simultaneously have an incentive to produce more. The reduced demand and increased supply are natural market forces that hold prices down. Not so in health care. Price signals are obscured by government interference, creating a wedge between consumers and suppliers. This wedge leads to overconsumption and a misallocation of resources. When the government spends money on health care or, through tax preferences, causes third parties to spend, the patient is separated from the transaction because costs are no longer his or her concern.

The length of the separation between the consumer and the supplier defines the size of the wedge. The larger the wedge, the more the dysfunction. It's common sense.

In 1960, before Medicare, more than 75 percent of total health-care expenditures in the United States were funded by private means.[1] As of 2007, this figure has declined to slightly more than 50 percent of total national health-care expenditures. Under Obamacare, this figure will literally collapse, as the private market will be completely crowded out. This wedge has been exacerbated by the fact that private-sector payments have been pushed to third parties because of the tax preference. When the private sector paid 75 percent of health-care costs, individuals paid nearly half of these costs from their own pockets. Today, the private sector funds a little more than half of all expenditures, and individual patients cover just $1 of every $10 spent on health care. Do the math: it's simple. The private sector makes about 50 percent of health-care expenditures, and individuals feel only 10 percent of this. That works out to 5 percent. That's a pretty big wedge. No wonder we have a cost problem. No wonder we have an uninsured problem.

The wedge reduces the incentives to produce and innovate, so we get less production and innovation. Yet at the same time, the wedge increases the incentives to consume and spend, since the cost of consumption is not borne by the one making the decision. Such basic economics cannot be repealed, any more than gravity.

So if Obamacare is not overturned by the Supreme Court, it should be repealed.

Because progressives think we're stupid, we are stuck with higher costs and less efficiency. Under our present system, inefficient delivery is subsidized at the expense of efficient delivery. Obamacare doubles down on this flaw.

This government interference, like nearly all government interference, hurts the poor more than it helps them. First, the tax distortions suppress cash wages. By driving costs higher, these distortions make care less affordable. The only way to get such a rich government subsidy is to have a job, but the out-of-control costs increase the cost of hiring a worker. If the cost of hiring a worker exceeds the value of that worker's productivity, which is more likely the case among the least skilled, the job is eliminated. The poor are always the ones to bear the heaviest burden of bad government policies.

These distortions have compounded for over fifty years. More of the same won't work. Tinkering won't work. Trimming around the edges won't work. Repeal of the tax code and the other twisted laws is the only option.

If we want to work on the right problem, we must eliminate the tax exclusion for employer-provided health insurance, which is one of the things 9-9-9 does. But that's not all. 9-9-9 replaces 5 taxes (corporate income tax code, personal income tax code, both employer and employee share of payroll taxes, the capital gains tax, and the death tax) with a 9 percent business flat tax, a 9 percent personal flat tax, and a 9 percent national sales tax.

Once we defeat Obama and repeal whatever may be left of Obamacare, health care is an easier fix than most people think.

Any reform that doesn't start by leveling the playing field will not work. Make it more like auto insurance. The top four auto insurers spend over $1 billion each year on advertising to tell us how to save money with their insurance. Have you ever heard of such commercials from a health insurance company?

Once we eliminate the wedge, I bet we'll have cavemen and lizards on TV constantly telling us how much we can save on health insurance. We have already seen the success of consumer-driven health care with Lasik eye surgery and contact lenses. Since neither was covered by insurance, each was immune to the distortion caused by the current system and instead faced market forces, which drove costs down, improved quality, and expanded access. Moving to a full consumer-driven model will solve most of the problems and at considerably less cost.

Nothing, of course, will solve all problems at once. Only lies claim to do that. Why not achieve the most improvement for the least cost and see what, if any, issues remain? If we did that, we would then be in a position to attack the remaining problems from a position of strength.

Trusting the American People Is the Key to Prosperity

The natural state of our economy is prosperity. Individuals try to do better each year, thanks to our God-given "unalienable Rights" to life, liberty, and the pursuit of happiness, as set out in the Declaration of Independence. All families strive to improve their situation each year based on what the American dream means to them. All businesses want to grow each year. I have never sat in a board of directors meeting where the discussion was centered on "how do we do worse?" or "how do we get smaller?" If these millions of entities, widely diffused throughout the economy, are all moving independently but in the direction of growth, the government is the only entity capable of exerting enough force to negate those collective efforts and result in stagnation or decline.

If government is limited, there will be prosperity. When government power is not constrained, prosperity suffers.

Next year will be the hundredth anniversary of both the Federal Reserve and the Internal Revenue Service. I won't be celebrating. In the eighty years prior to their creation, government was limited, and prosperity was the natural state of the economy. Growth averaged 4.25 percent over eighty years![2] Let me say that again. We grew at 4.25 percent for eighty years. By comparison, in the last decade we have had only two quarters in which growth exceeded 4.25 percent!

Just as impressive, prices were stable during this period, ending approximately where they began eighty years earlier. Then something happened. The Progressive Era gave us both the Fed and the IRS, and prosperity has never been the same. In fact, there have been fewer periods of sustained growth, less overall growth, less price stability, more financial crises, and less prosperity than before.

In Chapter 3, I offer a review of how the policies of Harding-Coolidge, Kennedy, Reagan, and Clinton promoted prosperity. The formula for each was to tame the twin evils of high taxes and an unstable dollar by lowering taxes and stabilizing our currency. It should be no wonder that the solutions offered by this book focus so heavily on rolling back the IRS and the Fed. Not to be left out, the whole regulatory apparatus has grown out of control and is also now in need of major reform. These three entities can be thought of as the "axis of evil" when it comes to economic growth and prosperity.

Figure 1-3 not only sums up the frustration of the people but holds the key to the answers.

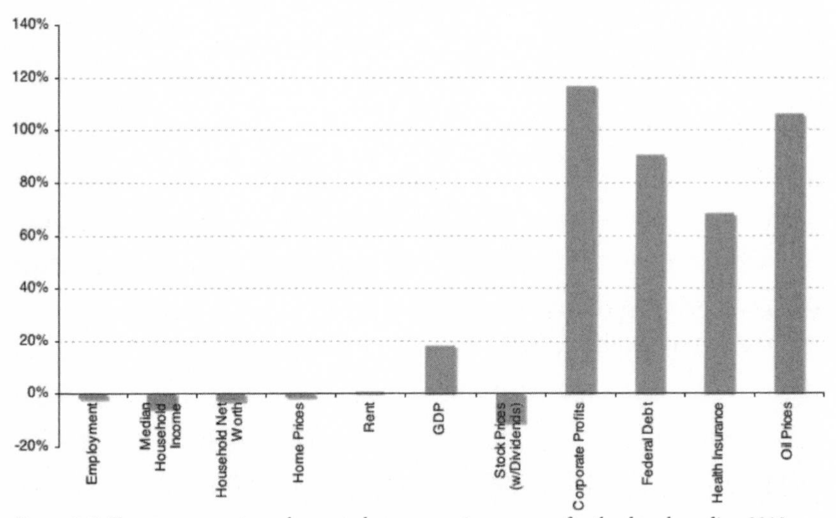

Figure 1-3. Ten-year percentage change in key economic measures for the decade ending 2010. (Department of Numbers. http://www.deptofnumbers.com/blog/2011/01/ten-years/

Notice that the economy—GDP, the center bar—has grown less than a paltry 20 percent in the last decade. The bars to the left of GDP show losses in employment, median household income, household net worth, and home prices. Is it any wonder people are frustrated? To the right of GDP are those areas that have been taking larger and larger shares of GDP. Corporate profits, government debt, health insurance, and oil prices have increased substantially, ranging from almost 70 percent to nearly 120 percent over the same span.

Here is the same data in table format.

Table 1-1

Ten-Year Changes in Broad Economic Measures

Change in Numbers

	Period Ending	From	To	% Change
Employment	Dec. 2010	132,347,000	130,539,000	1.37
Median household income	Dec. 2009	$52,388	$49,777	4.98
Household net worth	Sept. 2010	$55,957.73B	$54,891.17B	1.91
Home prices (Index)	Sept. 2010	134.27	133.22	0.79
Rent (OER Index)	Nov. 2010	255.391	257.192	0.71
GDP	Sept. 2010	$11,267.867B	$13,278.515B	17.84
S&P 500 Index	Dec. 2010	140.53	125.75	10.52
Corporate profits	Sept. 2010	$645.59B	$1,416.3B	119.38
Federal debt	Dec. 2010	$7,267.79B	$13,834.92B	90.36
Health insurance (family)	Dec. 2010	$8,180	$13,770	68.33
Oil prices	Nov. 2010	$41.36	$85.28	106.20

Source: Department of Numbers, http://www.deptofnumbers.com.

Keep in mind that corporate profits refer to corporations, while 80 to 90 percent of businesses are S corporations or partnerships paying taxes under the personal tax return and not the corporate return. Thus, the strong growth in the "corporate profits" category is not a barometer of business health in general, but rather an indication of the strength of large corporations. This speaks to the uneven playing field that hurts small business. Call me skeptical, but could it be that in return for acquiescence to massive regulations, beginning with the Sarbanes-Oxley Act of 2002, major corporations get the corporate tax code carved into Swiss cheese, resulting in a lower effective tax rate and a better cost of capital only for them?

During its first three years in office, the Obama administration unleashed 106 new major regulations that increased regulatory burdens by more than $46 billion annually, five times the amount imposed by the George W. Bush administration during its first three years.

Hundreds more costly new regulations are in the pipeline, many of which stem from the Dodd-Frank financial regulation statute and Obamacare. Small businesses in particular are under siege. The National Federation of Independent Business conducted a survey of small businesses in December 2011. The number of small businesses citing "regulations and red tape" as their single biggest problem jumped 26 percent in recent years and is now second only to "poor sales." These regulations crush small businesses, whereas large corporations have the critical mass to cope with the extra regulatory burden, particularly since this cost is offset by corporate tax breaks available to them but not available to their small-business counterparts, most of whom file under the personal return.

As a result, after-tax profit margins for corporations are at an all-time high (see Fig. 1-4).

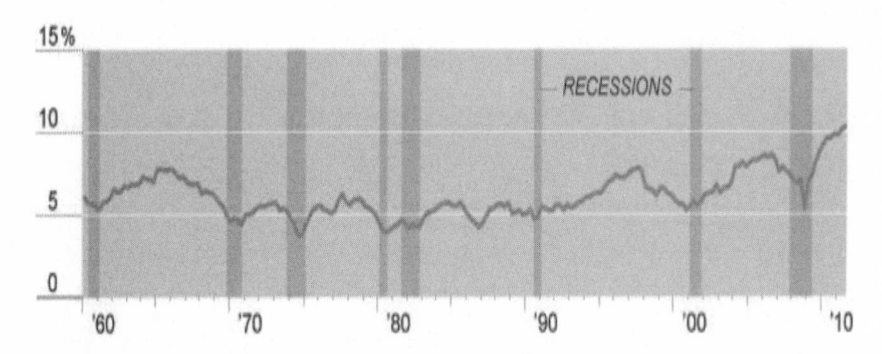

Figure 1-4. After-Tax Corporate Profits as a Percentage of GDP, 1960–2010. (Real-World Economics Review Blog, http://rwer.wordpress.com/2011/12/27/us-corporate-profits-after-tax-as-a-percentage-of-gdp/

It has been widely publicized that thirty well-known companies have collectively earned $163 billion in profit, paid $475 million to lobbyists, and paid zero income tax. (see TBL 1-2)

Table 1-2
U.S. Profits, Federal Income Taxes Paid, and Lobbying Expenses, 2008–2010

Company	**U.S. Profits ($ millions)**	**Taxes* ($ millions)**	**Lobbying ($ millions)**
General Electric	10,460	-4,737	84.35
PG&E	4,855	-1,027	78.99
Verizon Communications	32,518	-951	52.34
Wells Fargo	49,370	-681	11.04
American Electric Power	5,899	-545	28.85
Pepco Holdings	882	-508	3.76
Computer Sciences	1,666	-305	4.39
CenterPoint Energy	1,931	-284	2.65
NiSource	1,385	-227	1.83
Duke Energy	5,475	-216	17.47
Boeing	9,735	-178	52.29
NextEra Energy	6,403	-139	9.99
Consolidated Edison	4,263	-127	1.79
Paccar	365	-112	.76
Integrys Energy Group	818	-92	.71
Wisconsin Energy	1,725	-85	2.45
DuPont	2,124	-72	13.75
Baxter International	926	-66	10.45
Tenet Healthcare	415	-48	3.43
Ryder System	627	-46	.96
El Paso	4,105	-41	2.94
Honeywell International	4,903	-34	18.30
CMS Energy	1,292	-29	3.48
Con-way	286	-26	2.29
Navistar International	896	-18	6.31
DTE Energy	2,551	-17	4.37
Interpublic Group	571	-15	1.30
Mattel	1,020	-9	.84
Corning	1,977	-4	2.81
FedEx	4,247	37	50.81
Total	163,691	-10,602	475.67

Source: Profit and tax data: "Corporate Tax Payers and Corporate Tax Dodgers, 2008–10," Citizens for Tax Justice, November 2011; lobbying expenditure data: Center for Responsive Politics.
*A negative number indicates that the company paid "less than zero" in the sense that it received back from the government the value represented by the negative figure.

While they haven't done anything illegal, it is a symbol of our broken system. No wonder they don't use their clout to stand up and speak out against all of the burdensome regulations.

9-9-9 puts all businesses on a level playing field so that large corporations can't use their resources to take advantage of the complicated tax code while small ones struggle to just get by.

We already discussed health care and what has to be done to rein in costs. The fix is simpler than you might think. Because of its strong growth relative to GDP, compensation that would otherwise flow to employees gets eaten up by higher health-care costs. Figure 1-5 best captures the pain felt by most families. It shows where median family income is compared with where it should be if it tracked GDP per capita.

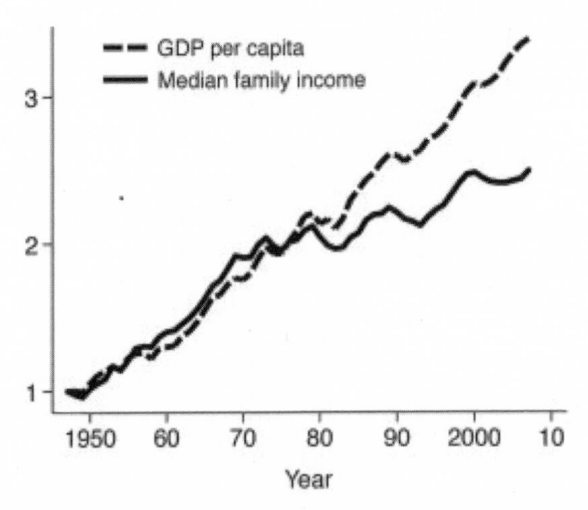

Figure 1-5. the decoupling of economic growth and middle-class income growth, 1950–2010. (Lane Kenworthy, "Is Decoupling Real?" Consider the Evidence, March 11, 2012, http://lanekenworthy.net/2012/03/11/is-decoupling-real/.)

Families produce GDP for businesses, yet their share in terms of income hasn't kept pace with their productivity. Families are working harder and harder, as evidenced by a growing GDP line, but feel as if their household economy is not keeping pace with the national economy. That is because it is not. The broken health-care system is part of this.

The other part has to do with the broken monetary system, which is the third reform addressed by the Cain Solutions Revolution. Ever since the sound money era ended in 1971, we have had a Federal Reserve that, for the most part, has treated wage growth as inflationary. We need to tell the Fed loud and clear that wage growth is a sign of prosperity, something that we want. The Fed's focus should not be to extinguish it. When we pass 9-9-9, I am certain we will see strong wage growth. But without a return to sound money, it would likely be only a matter of time before the Fed tried to stamp it out just as it was beginning to reach every corner of the country—particularly the areas that need it the most.

In Chapter 7, I explain this in more detail, making a case for monetary reform and presenting a specific solution for getting us there.

The politicians have messed up the tax code, the regulatory bureaucracy, and the monetary system so severely we are beyond the point of tinkering and fine-tuning. We need a major overhaul. The forces in the political class intentionally distort capitalism so they can blame capitalism and then grab more power. They always grab power through the tax code, the regulatory bureaucracy, and the monetary system—so this is where we must stop them. This approach of throwing sand in the gears and then blaming the engine is putting our country on the road to ruin.

My experience at Whirlpool helped me to see firsthand how the tax code bias ships jobs overseas. 9-9-9 fixes that. My experience at the Fed taught me how to fix the Fed. Although my resume indicates my paychecks were signed by large corporations, the franchisees I served were all small businesses, and I feel more of a kindred spirit to them. The best check and balance on big business is a bunch of hungry small competitors competing on a level playing field. It is either that or the way we're headed: to an uneven playing field that consolidates more control in the hands of fewer corporations, which in turn are under greater control by the government.

All three of my reforms transfer power from the big business, big government alliance to the people and level the playing field for small business.

Having trust in the people seems to come easily to most of us, but not to progressives. The major difference between conservatives and progressives is how each defines "average American." To a progressive, the average American can be determined by creating an imaginary line consisting of all 311 million Americans. The smartest are at the front of the line (they always place themselves in front), and the least smart are at the back of the line. Progressives, of course, believe they are the only ones capable of knowing exactly how to rank the rest of us.

They then proceed to the exact middle of the line, the 50th percentile. They remove this "average American" from the line and decide whether this single individual knows as much as the progressives know. They contemplate whether this single representative of the "unwashed masses" could possibly know as much as they do about all sorts of arcane issues. To progressives, it is safe to presume that government knows better than this middle American guy. This leads to redistribution, expansion of government, and loss of liberty. The result is subpar growth. (Note that I am careful to use the term "progressive" rather than "liberal." This is because there are many progressives within the Republican Party, and focusing only on differences between conservatives and liberals lets Republicans off the hook for the considerable damage done by the progressive wing of their party.)

Conservatives, on the other hand, think of the 311 million people in the aggregate as representing the "average American." E pluribus unum means "out of many, one." That's my definition of the average American. If we use this perspective, the average American is awesome, brilliant, and has all the answers for all of our problems. This body of people is capable of the most complex calculus under the sun. It appreciates the beauty and value of self-governance. The average American is a very capable individual if we get the government off our collective back, out of our pockets, and out of our way. The conservative view shows confidence that people know what is best for themselves.

To illustrate the difference, let's assume that I am a contestant on the game show Who Wants to Be a Millionaire. I am facing the smartest person the progressives can find to put up against me. Will it be Tim Geithner? One of the many all-knowing government czars? Eric Holder? King Obama himself? If I have an unlimited lifeline to all of you, the American people, I don't care how smart my opponent is, I will win every time. I will have every answer I need.

In Chapter 2 we will review the basic principles that can be used anywhere and at all times to better understand the economy in a simple, commonsense way. The key to understanding these principles is trust in the American people. Everything must pass the Uncle Leroy and Aunt Bessie test. My philosophy is this: if you can't explain things in simple terms that everyone can understand, you don't know your subject well enough. Too often, the political elites make things sound more complicated than they are because they want you to be both impressed and confused—impressed at how smart they must be, and confused enough to go along with their nice-sounding plans (which usually result in the opposite of what they promise). That's because they think you're stupid.

Sometimes the government numbers get so big they are difficult to comprehend. When that happens, I start chopping off digits until the number approaches a size more in relation to a family's finances. Thus, government spending of $3,600,000,000,000 ($3.6 trillion) can be reduced by eight zeros to $36,000, a number most people can relate to. If you cut eight digits off all the federal numbers, it stays an apples-to-apples comparison.

Using this approach, we see that the government's complex finances, reduced by eight digits, would be comparable to a family earning $23,000 per year but spending $36,000 per year. The spending exceeds the income by $13,000 per year, creating a deficit that gets added to the credit card each month. Oh, by the way, the credit card already has a balance due of $150,000! Do you remember the big fuss they had in Washington over how much spending to cut? Using the numbers the politicians argued over endlessly, they ultimately agreed to cut the equivalent of $300!

I trust that the American people are capable of understanding the seriousness of our problems. Meanwhile, the politicians have divided us more than ever, making the problem seem larger than it really is. Dividing the country is only beneficial to the forces that want to grow government and keep taking away your liberty. To solve the problems, we must unite. I am convinced there is more that unites us than divides us, and that it is easier to take the next step if it comes from common ground.

For example, we must reject the false premise that is put before us regarding the whole spending debate. If we allow the debate to be framed as whether we spend or cut, that can be too easily turned into a notion of whether or not to help people. Reject that premise. Of course we should help people. We should advocate the best way to help people.

In my business career, I found that the way to solve a problem is to involve those closest to the source of it. Trust the people. All help should be looked at from the perspective of the person needing the help. Clearly, it is best to empower these people to help themselves. That often costs less and is more likely to eliminate the problem. Next, strengthen the family, which is the next-closest unit. Strong families mean strong communities. Government power should be kept closest to the people at the state and local levels, not transferred to where it is least effective.

If there is a problem, who is best equipped to solve it? Would you look to a massive institution far from the problem itself—the one that is largest, slowest, most bureaucratic, and least informed about the people who actually need the help? Would you look to the entity that is least capable of caring or loving and has the strongest financial incentive to perpetuate the problem? That's the federal government. Yet some people automatically think of the federal government first when it comes to helping people.

We should trust people, families, and communities to solve problems. And they could, and would, if we get the federal government out of their way.

We should start by taking all federal spending that is not specifically authorized by the Constitution and ask, "Would people be helped more if these resources were deployed closer to the source of the problem?" One way to cut federal spending while still helping people is to redirect functions back to the states and local communities. This way, if government is inefficient, wasteful, ineffective, and corrupt, at least you can vote with your feet and move. More likely, with competition, good practices will get adopted faster and bad ones discarded as fast. Trust the people!

The gas tax should be levied by states only. Washington doesn't need to be involved with it. Why send it there only to have states lobby to get it back? Let the states keep it and decide how to reinvest it back into roads, bridges, and other transportation—or return it to the taxpayer. The Department of Education could be eliminated and the funds sent directly to the states, which in turn should send the bulk of them to the communities. This doesn't mean that I don't value education. Of course I do. Rather, it means I trust those closer to the action to have a bigger say in how those funds are best deployed. The work of the EPA, the Department of Energy, the Department of Commerce, FEMA, Housing, Food Stamps, Medicaid, and more agencies could be better handled at the state level, where we engage fifty laboratories of experimentation, all competing to try to deliver more value for less. When does a monopoly provider of anything ever offer the best combination of price and value?

This mind-set—of focusing on the best way to help people—makes it clear that the federal government should be limited. This will lead to a long overdue transfer of power back to the people. The result will be more progress in solving problems and more liberty for We the People.

The overriding theme of the problems we face is that the federal government has simply become too big and too powerful. The irony is that every penny of every government program at every level of government is paid for by the private sector. So why would it ever make sense to harm the private sector? If you tax people pulling the wagon and pay people to ride it, pretty soon the wagon stalls. That's where we are now. We have reached a tipping point where there is only one thing left to do: revolt.

We must overcome the divisions inflicted upon us. Our country is divided more than at any time in recent memory, more than we desire and deserve, and more than we can tolerate if we are to solve the major challenges facing us. We are divided between those who want to spend and those who want to cut. My solution is to unite around growth. We are divided between those who want to eliminate deductions and those who want to reduce tax rates. My solution accomplishes both. But more important than that, the country is divided between those who believe Washington is fine but America needs to be fundamentally transformed and those of us who believe America will be just fine once we fundamentally transform Washington.

This divide is best symbolized by the wall that separates those with ideas from those with capital. It makes no sense to wall off people with ideas. They are the ones who give us innovation, new business formation, job creation, and wealth generation. President Obama wants to continue building this wall higher because it satisfies his impulse to punish capital. But he is completely unaware that it is those people with ideas, who need capital, whom he harms the most. Without capital, Steve Jobs was just another dreamer.

On one side of the wall are entrepreneurs. Among them is the next Steve Jobs, who will find better solutions to our energy problems than government bureaucrats could ever hope to find. The combination of science, technology, and the American spirit will tap our abundance of clean American energy—red, white, and blue energy—if we allow it. Entrepreneurs in the health-care sector, using different science and technology but the same American spirit, will cure diseases and prove they can drive costs down better than bureaucratic rationing. If only we allow it.

These are the people ready to bust loose with all kinds of innovation that will create economic growth and improve America's quality of life. And they're looking up at the wall.

This wall is composed of a tax code that punishes capital formation. And it chases away the capital that does form. What's left, it double-taxes. The wall, and all activity around it, is guarded by regulators who hinder, threaten, and intimidate the coming together of ideas with capital—and do so under nearly every circumstance, as though this coming together were a hostile act. The wall is fortified by an unstable monetary system that diverts capital away from job-creating investments because it must be used instead to hedge against the debasement of the dollar and the financial chaos it causes.

The millions who are unemployed, underemployed, or so discouraged they have dropped out of the labor force—along with the entrepreneurs upon whom their livelihood depends—cannot understand how demonizing those on the other side of the wall helps them or anyone else.

Because it doesn't.

People who, like President Obama, don't trust the American people and think they should use the power of the federal government to "fundamentally transform this country" make it their life's work to keep adding to the wall, brick by brick, relentlessly. For all of you who believe, as I do, that the American people will be better off—our economy stronger, our liberty restored, our families more prosperous, our position in the world more secure—if we fundamentally transform Washington, please join me in demanding:

MR. PRESIDENT, TEAR DOWN THIS WALL!

The Solutions Revolution is about transferring power back to the people, where it belongs. This book is devoted to proposing specific solutions to generate the conditions necessary for growth and prosperity that will make America the world's leader well into the next century.

If we don't prevail, we will, as Ronald Reagan said, spend our sunset years telling our children and grandchildren what America was like when it was a free country.

Tearing down this wall will transfer power from Washington, D.C., back to the people, where it belongs. By replacing the tax code, 9-9-9 will engineer the largest transfer of power from Washington to the people in the history of the Republic. Setting up a Regulatory Budget Office will force government to be accountable for the real-life impact of the regulations it seeks to impose. This, too, will represent an enormous transfer of power from previously unaccountable bureaucrats to the people. And restoring a sound money system through my monetary reform, the 21st Century Gold Standard, will bring about the biggest transfer of power from the Federal Reserve to the people in the history of the republic.

We must harness the collective wisdom of the American people and get behind solutions. The Boston Tea Party of 1773 led to a revolution against power-hungry elites. Today's Tea Party movement must also lead a revolution, but this time the weapon of choice will be solutions. Those in the Occupy movement should take a look at our ideas. It may surprise them at first, but many of their concerns are addressed by our solutions.

The common pattern is that every solution offered here transfers power from the government back to the people. The Cain Solutions Revolution is here. It is time to take our power back!

Chapter 2

The Right Diagnosis Yields the Right Cure

In disquisitions of every kind, there are certain primary truths, or first principles, upon which all subsequent reasonings must depend.

—Alexander Hamilton, Federalist No. 31, January 1, 1788

It seems that we live in a time when folks are divided into camps, and the camps can't agree with each other on anything. Even the weather can be fodder for a political argument.

In an environment like that, can it ever be possible for the country to unite behind real solutions to its most pressing problems? It can—if effective leaders successfully rally the nation around basic principles upon which everyone can agree.

Uniting around basic principles will demonstrate that we have common ground on which to begin designing solutions. And it's necessary that we do this. If someone believes the world is flat but I don't, we are not going to agree on the next steps. We will never reconcile our differences until we establish common ground with common principles.

The principles we use here are as elementary as gravity and just as immutable. In fact, it doesn't require anything complicated to solve our problems, just a willingness to find common principles. The progressive elites, who think they know better, make things complicated on purpose, as if to show us how much we need their keen counsel. To conceal the absurdity of their ideas, they cloak them in complexity and hope the average American will not understand. If progressives ever advocated getting rid of gravity, I don't care how much good they might claim it will do humanity, people will know better. We ain't stupid! Progressives prey on our compassion because they know we have a heart, but they think we have no brain. To a conservative, in order to have a warm heart, a person must first have clear eyes.

Economic Growth Is the Answer

Why is economic growth so important? Picture a world consisting of two people, you and me. I raise cattle and you grow vegetables. Assume we don't trade. The economy is zero. As soon as we decide to trade our produce (notice we have to produce before we can consume), we are both better off. We both have more balanced diets and less spoilage. The amount by which we are better off is measured by the volume of trade between us, and the volume of trade measures the economy.

Since trade is voluntary, by definition it is mutually beneficial. Unless both parties believe they are better off, at least one party will decline to trade. As a society, expanding voluntary trade by definition improves living standards and makes society better off. This is why it is so important to measure output (that is, gross domestic product, or GDP). It measures the extent to which we are better off.

Our focus should be on expanding output as much as possible, which means government should be as restrained as possible. The only party capable of initiating involuntary trade is the government, and such efforts highly distort the economy and reduce living standards.

For output to expand, the government must get off our backs, out of our way, and out of our pockets. I am reminded of a quotation from Ronald Reagan about the mind-set of government: "If it moves, tax it. If it keeps moving, regulate it. And if it stops moving, subsidize it."

If every penny of every government program at every level of government is paid for by the private sector, why does the Obama administration have a hostile attitude toward the private sector? A strong private sector should be our number one objective. Want a strong national defense? Start with a strong economy. Want to create jobs? Start with a strong economy. Want to increase living standards? Start with a strong economy. Want to help the poor, restrain spending, and fix Social Security? Start with a strong economy. Do you see a trend?

Our problems are not insurmountable by any stretch. They simply require the right action. The right results will flow from the right action. Under Obama, we are getting exactly the results you should expect from the wrong action. This is not unique to Obama. Anyone who follows the wrong action will get the wrong results.

This is not complicated. Only the elites think our problems are too complicated. Social Security can be fixed by getting our economic growth rate above 3.5 percent and indexing benefits to inflation instead of wage growth. Problem solved. I will briefly discuss in Chapter 5 how 9-9-9 is designed to accommodate a personal retirement option for Social Security like the one they have in Chile.

I don't expect the nation's elites to embrace that idea, but I'm not talking to them in this book. They are not going to lead in the embrace of these solutions because (1) they don't want to, and (2) it would take too long for them to unlearn all the things they know that just ain't so. My message is intended for all the people like Uncle Leroy and Aunt Bessie, who will be happy to embrace these basic principles and, when turned into an Army of Davids, will demand that the elites either take the right actions or step aside so others can. The elites got us into this mess, and we will take care of who matters most: We the People.

Cain's Three Economic Guiding Principles

1. Production, Not Spending, Drives the Economy

If you wonder how progressives in Washington can defend more than $1 trillion in deficit spending every year, you have to realize that they are convinced this spending is essential for the economy. In their world, massive federal spending is the best thing you can do to spur economic growth.

They're wrong. Only production drives economic growth. There is nothing more fundamental in all of economics than this essential truth.

Consider that we all have to produce first, in order to get paid second, so that we may consume third. Don't let the progressives play that chicken-and-egg game with you. They will say, "But you need demand, too. You can't supply anything unless there is consumer demand." They think you're stupid. If you were stranded on an uninhabited island, how would you consume? Could you consume simply because you demanded it? Of course not! You would have to produce first. If you want to consume fish, first you must catch one. If you want to consume fruit, first you must go pick some. It is the act of producing that drives the economy. You produce so you can voluntarily exchange with others, which allows you to consume.

The whole notion that consumption drives the economy is kept alive by those who want to use it as a rationale to redistribute income. Consumption is only relevant in that it helps to measure what has been produced. Production pulls along consumption the way an engine pulls a caboose. Just because they are traveling at the same speed doesn't for one second mean that the caboose is pushing the train down the tracks.

If something is wrong with the economy, fix the production (or supply) side. Policies that attempt to stimulate the consumption (or demand) side are equivalent to putting fuel in the caboose. With record "stimulus" spending by Obama, it is no surprise that the economy is stalled. All of it went into the caboose. No amount of fuel will help if it's put in the caboose. And think about how much valuable fuel was wasted that could have been fed into the engine.

This principle is about more than just economics. Society's supply-first mind-set says, "I must serve the needs of others before I can satisfy my own." The consumption-first mind-set is just the opposite. It says putting your needs first is the only objective. That drives the greed and materialism that are counter to traditional values. The ruse that consumption drives the economy exists only to serve as a rationale for every redistribution scheme known to humanity.

Once you produce, you can do no harm to society. If you spend all you produce, your spending translates into income for all the merchants. If you save, you increase bank deposits, which in turn increase loan capacity for other producers who want to expand production and need access to loans. If you invest, you lower the cost of capital for all firms seeking to expand.

When the government spends, it has the opposite effect. That is because the government must take from the production of others in order to redistribute it. It is true that the recipient of the government spending spends the money, and that becomes income to the merchant. With the extra income, that merchant spends, and so on, thus unleashing what economists call the multiplier effect.

The only problem, which is true with most progressive theories, is that it doesn't go far enough. As Thomas Sowell says, we must "think beyond stage one." Because the next stage, which the progressives always leave out, is that the person whose income was taken (that is, taxed) will spend less. And the merchant whom the taxpayer would otherwise buy from will have less income, and so on down the line, thus unleashing a negative multiplier effect. The two "spending effects" completely cancel each other out. The incentive effects, however, are permanent. Effort that would otherwise be directed toward expanding output is thus redirected toward avoiding the tax instead. The result is less output for society.

Government spending is equivalent to taking a bucket of water out of the deep end of the swimming pool and pouring it in the shallow end—then hoping the water level will change.

That is what the president meant by hope and change. 9-9-9 is a tax system that encourages production by shifting the burden to consumption. Further, because of the way it exempts investment, it is functionally equivalent to a full consumption tax.

2. Risk-Taking Drives Growth

To expand output, somebody somewhere has to take a risk. Progressives think that companies get started because someone demands it. Nonsense. If demand comes first, how did Facebook get created? Because someone demanded it? Did a bunch of consumers get together and tell the founders what their demands were? No, a producer had an idea and got together with investors who were willing to risk their capital. Although the founders could have been motivated by altruism, the financiers who put up the capital, like every investor, were focused on after-tax returns. There was no guarantee of positive results. Once production has taken place, demand will meet it if the product is successful. If it is not successful, it should fail—so others can learn by it—and not get bailed out. What if we had the bailout-nation mind-set when Edison invented the lightbulb? His thousands of initial failures would have been bailed out and subsidized, protecting the failures and setting back technological progress.

While a producer anticipates demand before coming up with new products or a new business, there is no assurance that the hoped-for demand will arise. The producer takes that risk. Without that risk, there are no new companies or new products.

Risk-taking is not limited to entrepreneurs. They take the biggest risks, but all of us take risks each day. Most of us (actually millions fewer under Obama) go to work and work hard in hopes of a raise or a bonus. Risk is the expenditure of effort with an expectation of reward, but with no guarantee that the reward will come.

Because there is a virtually unlimited supply of new ideas, growth is typically constrained by factors that influence the amount of capital willing to finance ideas. The wall that separates capital from ideas has to be torn down in order to sustain a high growth rate. The tax code is hostile to the coming together of capital and ideas, the regulatory bureaucracy suffocates it, and the monetary system is so unstable that it drives massive amounts of capital into hedges and safe havens, all at the expense of ideas that go unfunded.

Regulations have become so complex and burdensome, so discretionary in their application and arbitrary in their enforcement, that they represent a risk factor which no business can quantify, let alone plan for. The Regulatory Budget Office will cap and quantify this impact, providing necessary certainty to producers.

3. Measurements Must Be Dependable

Imagine what life would be like if you had to wake up in the morning and check the newspaper to find out if an hour was still made up of sixty minutes or if a foot still equaled twelve inches. Life would be utter chaos. Life as we know it would be impossible. Without a standard of fixed measurements, you could not go anywhere or do anything with any confidence. But that is exactly what we allow the politicians to do with the most important unit of measure in the world: the dollar. By letting the dollar "float," politicians leave it unanchored to reliability.

All of your income, all of your belongings, and your entire life's savings are denominated in dollars. When the dollar loses its value, it is a direct confiscation of your income and net worth. The reason politicians like this form of redistribution so much is that most people don't see it, and they can always claim plausible deniability and blame the Federal Reserve.

Another lie told by the progressives is that "market forces" determine the dollar. Don't you just love how the very people who despise market forces will use the term to cover up what really happens? Actually, the government, through its policies, determines the value of the dollar. The market simply reacts!

I never put such trickery past the politicians. That's what they do. But this clever smoke screen of blaming markets doesn't cover up the fact that the economy simply functions better with a dollar whose value is stable. In fact, the more complex a society is, the more it relies on fixed standards of measurement.

I served on the board of the Federal Reserve Bank of Kansas City, so I have some experience with both the good and the bad of the institution. The Kansas City Fed, by the way, has produced the two best policymakers that the Fed has ever had, in my opinion: former Kansas City Fed director Wayne Angell and former Kansas City Fed president Tom Hoenig, both of whom advocate a stable and reliable dollar. If all Fed policymakers were this good, we wouldn't have the problem we have now.

If the value of the dollar were really left to the market, the market would say in a loud voice that it always wants a stable and reliable unit of measure, as evidenced by the superior record of stronger economic growth, lower unemployment, fewer financial crises, and more widespread prosperity during periods when the dollar retained its value.

My monetary reform, the 21st Century Gold Standard, will restore this prosperity. Under it, a dollar will always retain its value in the same way an hour is always sixty minutes.

Tax the Broadest Possible Base at the Lowest Possible Rate

You realize where the government gets its money, right?

Every penny of every government program at every level of government is paid for by private-sector production. Why in the world would we do anything to harm private-sector production? Harming the private sector harms government, and those who rely upon it for its help. It makes no sense whatsoever, and helps no one, to torture those who constitute the private sector. Yet that is what our tax code does.

The government does not create resources; it merely redistributes them. So the goal should be to raise the requisite revenue while doing the least damage to the private sector that creates it.

The tax code in 2010 topped 71,000 pages. If it continues to expand at its historical rate, it will add, on average, 3,500 pages in the next administration. Where and when does it end? Every page is more torture for you but a gold mine for politicians. They use the tax code to control outcomes, create uneven playing fields to benefit their cronies, dole out special favors, reward campaign donors, and redistribute income. Guess who pays for this. We do, in the form of higher rates and more taxes.

Bankrate.com publishes the wackiest deductions taken each year from a survey of accountants. These are not deductions that are advisable to take—some border on the outrageous, but people take them. The tax code is so complex in some cases that it is hard for anyone to tell what is legitimate, and this invites some people to be highly creative. Guess who pays for this.

By the way, if you don't believe me, ask the IRS! Even it thinks the complexity of the tax code is out of control.

The IRS identified tax code complexity as the number one problem facing taxpayers.[3] In this same report the IRS recommended that Congress "substantially simplify" the Internal Revenue Code. Again in 2009, it reiterated its stance that complexity is the "most serious problem" and simplicity is important. In 2010, noting 4,428 tax changes over the last decade—including an estimated 579 changes in 2010 alone—the IRS said that tax complexity is still the number one problem.

But Congress isn't listening to us or to the IRS.

According to a recent study by the Laffer Center, tax code complexity imposes a burden on the private sector of $431 billion.[4] In addition to IRS administrative costs, this includes the cost of taxpayers spending 6.1 billion hours of their time, plus $31 billion in direct expenditures, on professional services and software programs. This works out to 30 cents for each dollar sent to the IRS—a 30 percent compliance premium. And this figure doesn't count the negative impact on the economy from a massive misallocation of resources, distortions of decision making, and reduced economic efficiency.

With all this complexity, it is impossible to achieve fairness no matter how you define it, so let's quit using the tax code for social engineering. The only thing this does consistently is destroy jobs, reduce output, and hurt wages.

So where is the best place to start in developing a better tax code?

All tax reform proposals must start with GDP and work their way down to determine the tax base. The tax base is the definition of which economic activity is subject to tax. Figure 2-1 shows the "circular flow" from Economics 101.

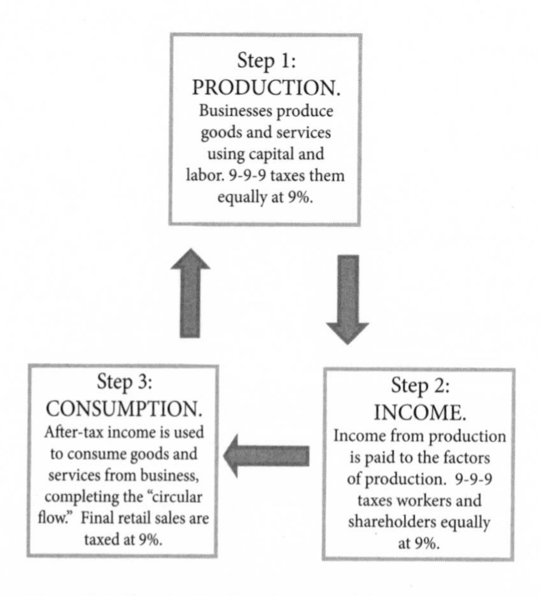

Figure 2-1. The circular flow diagram of the economy.

Taxing only one step in the flow, income, will result in a higher tax rate because the tax base is smaller. Higher tax rates discourage productive activity in favor of schemes to reduce taxable income. Taxing all three bases at the same rate is preferable since it offers the lowest rate, the least incentive to avoid paying taxes, and the fewest opportunities to do so. Chapter 5 is devoted to the benefits of this tax structure.

Low marginal tax rates on production drive incentives. The "marginal incentive" is the amount of money you keep of each additional dollar earned (expressed as 1 minus the tax rate). If your tax rate is 9 percent, it means you pay 9 cents of the next dollar you earn to taxes and keep 91 cents. Your incentive for producing another dollar is that you get to keep 91 cents of it. The marginal incentive is thus 91 percent.

Let's compare the change in incentives if we move from the current tax code to 9-9-9 and then contrast that with President Obama's plan to increase rates.

The current top tax rate is 35 percent, so the marginal incentive is 65 percent. Going from keeping only 65 cents on the dollar to keeping 91 cents—as 9-9-9 would do—is an increase of 40 percent! If people experience a 40 percent increase in what they will keep on the next dollar of output, there is a strong incentive to expand output. By contrast, Obama wants to raise taxes a lot. According to Wall Street Journal economics writer Stephen Moore, when all tax increases, surcharges, and so on are compiled, the marginal tax rate desired by Obama is 47.9 percent. This means a marginal incentive of only 52.1 percent.

What will help the economy more? Workers, innovators, entrepreneurs, and job creators keeping 91 cents on their next dollar—or only 52 cents? You don't have to be a math major to know that a 40 percent increase in the incentive to produce is better than a 20 percent reduction.

As a frame of reference, the Kemp-Roth tax cuts reduced rates from 70 percent to 50 percent. This meant producers got to keep 50 cents on the dollar after tax rather than 30 cents, for an increase in the marginal incentive of 67 percent. Reagan's 1986 tax reform reduced rates further from 50 percent to 28 percent, which changed marginal incentives from 50 percent to 72 percent, for an increase of 44 percent.

How can 9-9-9 lower rates that much? Easy. Eliminate complexity, simplify the tax code, and eliminate the thousands of pages of special deductions that cost the rest of us in the form of a much higher tax rate.

The biggest obstacle to true tax reform is that half of the country doesn't pay any federal income tax. But they pay plenty of payroll taxes: FICA, the Federal Insurance Contributions Act taxes for Social Security and Medicare. Thus, we have a counterproductive tug-of-war between payroll tax payers on one side and income tax payers on the other. Reducing the current system's income tax rates will generate economic growth by increasing marginal incentives, but doing so will meet political opposition because it only helps those on one side of the rope. Delivering relief to the payroll tax payers alone is wrong on two counts: First, it doesn't affect marginal tax rates for most of the economy, so it doesn't change marginal incentives much. Second, because it claims to "put money in people's pockets," it is based on the flawed theory that consumption drives the economy. (But as we discussed in the section on economic guiding principles, we know that the economy is driven by production, not consumption.) We need to unite all taxpayers instead of pulling against each other. Doing so not only expands the base, helping to get the rate lower; it also gives all of us the same incentive to keep rates low.

Principles of Tax Reform

These are the basic principles of tax reform:

Simplicity: If the tax code is simple, people will voluntarily comply. Complexity exerts a cost on society that reduces output.

Transparency: The more transparent taxes are, the more we know about the true cost of government. The more we all know about the true cost of government, the less government we will demand. The sales tax improves transparency, and transparency is our best defense against the progressive agenda, which tries at all times to raise any tax as much as possible.

Efficiency: What are compliance costs as a share of revenue collections? According to a Laffer Center study, the current tax code imposes a $431 billion deadweight on the economy in the form of compliance costs. This means it costs 30 cents just to send the IRS $1, a 30 percent compliance premium. Efficiency is maximized when compliance costs are minimal as a percentage of revenue collected. Aside from compliance costs, another measure of lost efficiency is the so-called tax gap, the amount the IRS actually collects compared with what it expects to collect. Estimates range from $300 million to $400 million annually. Rather than hire thousands of additional IRS agents to close this gap, as the administration has proposed, we should lay off thousands of IRS agents and implement 9-9-9. The gap will close itself.

Fairness: We should be treated the same, according to the dictionary definition of fairness, and Washington should not pick winners and losers through the tax code.

Fairness can be looked at horizontally and vertically. Horizontal fairness means people with similar incomes are treated equally. The current code treats people of the same income unequally by means of the many exemptions, deductions, credits, and other intricacies of the income tax. For example, the tax differences between homeowners and renters with the same incomes can be thousands of dollars because of itemized deductions for property taxes and mortgage interest.

Vertical fairness means people of different incomes are treated by the same principles of fairness. Vertical inequality of taxation violates the spirit of equal protection guarantees in the Constitution. Such unequal burdens distort perceptions about the costs and benefits of government because programs appear to be free of cost to many and unfairly costly to others. Under 9-9-9, all taxpayers are treated fairly.

Neutrality: The tax code should not create a bias that results in an uneven playing field. 9-9-9 is completely neutral. There are no uneven playing fields. Production and consumption are taxed equally. Capital and labor are taxed equally. Workers and shareholders are taxed equally. Exports and world goods are taxed equally. Imports and domestic goods are taxed equally. Small businesses and large businesses are taxed equally. Corporations and partnerships are taxed equally. Businesses and individuals both pay the same rate. Finally, businesses are taxed the same whether they pay dividends or retain earnings. This eliminates the double taxation of dividends. The present tax code exerts a counterproductive bias on all of these issues.

The Government "Wedge" Determines Employment

Figure 2-2 illustrates the tax wedge.

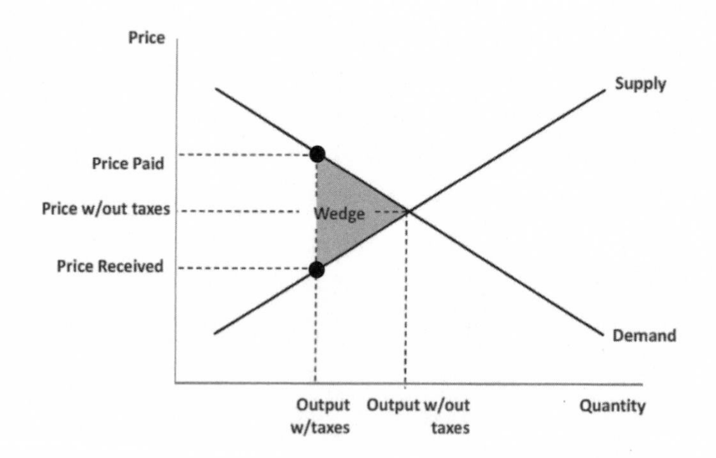

Figure 2-2. The tax wedge.

The downward sloping line represents the demand for labor. If productivity is constant, then the greater the cost to employ someone, the less demand there will be for labor. The upward sloping line is the supply of labor. If productivity is constant, workers will supply more labor at higher wages. "Price w/out taxes" shows the price to labor, assuming zero added tax costs. The result is marked by "Output w/out taxes."

From the employer's point of view, when taxes enter the picture, they increase the cost to employ a worker and reduce demand to the level marked by "Price Paid." From the employee standpoint, taxes reduce net wages received and result in less labor being supplied, as marked by "Price Received." Notice that output is lower at this level, as marked by "Output w/ taxes." This defines the tax wedge.

Quite simply, the tax wedge reduces employment, wages, and output. Reducing the tax wedge will increase employment, wages, and output. It's common sense.

This wedge concept can also be used to capture the cost of regulations. Regulations cost employers several thousand dollars per worker. This increases the cost to hire a worker, resulting in less demand for labor. As we will see in Chapter 6, the regulatory burden now actually exceeds the income tax burden. This adds significantly to the cost of hiring a worker. If that worker's productivity doesn't exceed the cost of hiring him or her, the job is eliminated.

The Capital-to-Labor Ratio Drives Wages

Wages are driven by productivity, and a worker will be more productive if more capital is invested in his or her efforts. Think of it this way: if your job is to dig a ditch, and your employer's investment is to equip you with a simple stick that costs $1, how productive will you be? Not very. If your employer equips you with a shovel that costs $10, you'll be much more productive—perhaps ten times more—and your wages will be higher. And if your employer equips you with a steam shovel that increases your productivity one hundred times more than that, your wages will be commensurately higher.

The more capital is invested in labor, the more productive labor will be, and the higher the wages workers can command.

During the 2008 presidential campaign, Barack Obama said: "Start rewarding work, and not just wealth." I was flabbergasted by his economic ignorance. Capital and labor are not at war with each other. Capital and labor need each other. They are joined at the hip.

Policy should be aimed at making capital plentiful relative to labor. 9-9-9 increases capital formation and makes it attractive for businesses to invest in their workers. An opposing view of the capital-to-labor ratio is to increase wages by making labor scarce relative to capital. That is what unions try to do. In both cases, the ratio may be the same, but the former is clearly preferable in terms of public policy.

We should strive to have as much capital invested per worker as possible. Businesses make capital investments for the explicit purpose of making their workforces more productive. Increased productivity is shared by the employee and the business (assuming that the government wedge hasn't increased).

But progressives attack this notion, thinking we need to save all the jobs of the old ditch-digging industry—the ones using shovels. Should we save these jobs? No. Look what happens throughout the rest of the economy if we don't. Some employment will shift to the manufacturer of steam shovels. These will be higher-value jobs. Further, because ditches will cost less, more ditch digging will occur. Employment will go up for construction, swimming pool installations, and all other ditch-digging-intensive industries. The money saved because of the decreased cost of digging ditches will be spent elsewhere, creating jobs in those areas. Otherwise, the money will be saved in the bank, where it increases bank deposits and thus bank loans, thereby increasing employment in the financial sector. Larry Kudlow, one of my favorite business commentators on TV, calls this process "creative destruction," a concept championed by his favorite economist, Joseph Schumpeter.

During the two decades from 1981 to 2000, a generally prosperous time by any standard, the number of jobs increased from 99 million to 137 million—an impressive increase of 38 million net new jobs. Notice I used the word "net." Job growth doesn't occur in a straight line. During this period, weekly claims for unemployment insurance also averaged 370,000. This means that in order to create 38 million net new jobs over two decades, on a weekly basis the economy had to create an average of 406,500 new jobs while simultaneously shedding 370,000 other jobs for a net increase of 36,500 new jobs per week. This way of looking at it gives you an idea of creative destruction at work, but also hopefully an appreciation of the fragile nature of employment.

You might not always have the job you have today, but that doesn't mean you won't be okay as long as the economy is growing.

If we put the concepts of the last two sections together, we can see one of the forces contributing to stagnant wages over the last decade. First, the government wedge explains how increases in taxes and regulations increase the cost to an employer of having employees. When productivity gains have to be used, in part, to offset an increase in the wedge, there is less benefit to the employee. No wonder many Americans feel as though they work harder and harder but don't receive fair, commensurate, and just rewards. They increase productivity each year just to keep pace with the government wedge, or else they lose their jobs. If the wedge were held constant, then productivity gains would benefit the worker. The best of both worlds would be to reduce the wedge and increase the capital-to-labor ratio significantly. That is precisely what 9-9-9 does.

Business Taxes Are Invisible Sales Taxes

Just because politicians tell you they're going to tax business doesn't mean business will bear the burden of that tax. Regardless of where politicians aim a tax, it is always paid by you, the general public.

Picture a farmer who marks up his product to cover all costs, including taxes, then passes those costs to the food processor, who likewise marks up the product, as do the distributor and the retailer. Who ends up paying these taxes? The guys at the end of the line. The consumers.

Having trouble visualizing this? Run it in reverse. Let's say you purchase something and hand over $1 to the convenience store cashier. That store keeps 25 cents, then pays its distributor 75 cents. The distributor keeps 25 cents, then pays 50 cents to the processor. The processor keeps 25 cents and pays the last 25 cents to the farmer. Each ends up with revenues of 25 cents from which to cover all costs, including taxes. Who ultimately pays these taxes? The consumer, who paid $1.

The taxes were supposedly levied on all these businesses, but the burden of the tax fell to consumers in the form of higher prices. Either way, consumers pay the tax. That's why every tax on business is really an invisible sales tax levied on the consumer.

The lack of visibility of the tax, however, is a problem. To illustrate, let's say that all taxes were directed at businesses and there was no income tax or sales tax. All those costs would be built into the prices of goods and passed along to consumers, but the tax burden would not be visible. The lack of visibility allows politicians to say with a straight face, "I won't raise your taxes; I will raise business taxes."

A visible tax is harder to raise than an invisible one. The more people we can unite under the same tax, and the more people who see that tax, the stronger the defense we have against an increase in the rate. When it comes to stopping the taxation Goliath, an Army of Davids is far stronger than a single David.

If $1 of business taxes is converted into $1 of sales taxes, overall taxes on consumers do not go up. One is a replacement for the other. The only thing that goes up is visibility. 9-9-9 capitalizes on this concept by converting invisible business taxes to visible sales taxes. This does not increase out-of-pocket costs to consumers. It only increases their awareness of the real taxes they pay. This is as basic as a free press and other protections of the Constitution. This is being informed. This is self-government. This is democracy.

The more we see the taxes we pay for everything, and the more we realize how much government really costs us, the less government we will demand and the better off all of us, from all walks of life, will be.

Chapter 3

The Right Way to Cut Taxes

> *The supply-side claim is not a claim. It is empirically true and historically convincing that with lower rates of taxation on labor and capital, the factors of production, you'll get a bigger economy.*
>
> *—Jack Kemp*

Stimulate Economic Growth

I'm all for tax cuts, but some tax cuts are more effective than others because they focus on the right things. If you want to spur economic growth by cutting taxes, you have to understand how to incentivize activity that leads to growth.

People work for after-tax income and invest for after-tax returns. Further, we respond to incentives, and changes in tax rates change incentives. Reductions in "marginal" tax rates—in other words, the tax rate that applies to the next, or marginal, dollar you earn—add to future income and thereby directly increase incentives for future production. Reductions in average (or effective) tax rates apply to income already earned and do not change future incentives.

If you receive a tax rebate check (as many did under Bush in 2001 and again in 2008, when then candidate Obama led the charge calling for them), it lowers your average tax rate but does not change your marginal tax rate. It has no impact on how you will be taxed on the next dollar you earn.

With no change in the incentive for future production, how will that increase future production? You're right, it won't. This type of tax cut is done for purely political reasons. The politicians claim that it "puts money in people's pockets." This is based on the failed theory that spending drives the economy. As we discussed in Chapter 2, this is false.

Sure, who would not want to receive a rebate check from the government? But when the private sector sends it a dollar, only to receive a rebate of the same dollar, that does nothing to stimulate the economy. This is nothing more than government spending disguised as a tax cut. If this worked as advertised, why stop with a few dollars? Why not have government tax 100 percent of GDP, then issue rebate checks to all? (Don't read that out loud! The Obama administration might overhear you and grab onto the idea.) GDP would quickly approach zero as there would be no reason to produce. The reason politicians do this is to redistribute income.

But redistribution doesn't work to stimulate the economy, either. If it did, once again, why not go all the way? If you taxed all income above the median income level at 100 percent, and sent rebate checks to those below the median income so that they were brought up to the median income level, we would all finally have equal income, at zero. (Thinking beyond stage 1, why would you work to earn the median income when you could choose to not work and receive the median income? The new median income would become zero.)

The other problem I have with tax cuts that change average rates rather than marginal rates is that they pollute the historical economic data on tax cuts. If the historical data on all tax cuts, good and bad, is presented by a "scholar," he or she can make a case that tax cuts do not work. My master's degree in computer science taught me that basic rule we all know: garbage in, garbage out. A "good unseparated from the bad" approach is the equivalent of a golf pro hitting twenty golf balls far and down the middle of the driving range followed by someone with lousy form hitting twenty more erratically. Then a "researcher" comes by and measures the distance and accuracy of all forty balls only to conclude that on average golf swings are erratic. Of course, form matters.

There are good tax cuts and bad tax cuts. Good ones are reductions in marginal tax rates on production. These include business income, personal income, capital gains, and estate taxes. The bad ones are reductions in average tax rates geared toward consumption.

Obama's payroll tax reduction is a good example. It has no impact on most people's marginal rate, so it reduces the tax on income already earned rather than on the next dollar earned. This will be a deadweight loss of revenue. It does reduce the marginal rate for some in the lower-income brackets, but not enough to make up for the loss. On balance, it will not be effective.

The real problem is that the country is artificially divided over the label applied to the tax paid. On one side of the tug-of-war, we have people who don't pay any income tax but pay lots of payroll taxes, pulling against those who pay not only payroll taxes but all of the income taxes. To cut marginal rates to help the economy is seen as benefiting only one side of the rope. To cut payroll taxes may help the other side of the rope, but it won't help the economy. 9-9-9 solves this problem by removing the artificial labels and uniting all taxpayers so we all pull together from the same side in favor of lower marginal rates.

We're going to look at examples of good tax cuts at work, but first, here are a few other factors to consider.

Size and Timing of Tax Cuts, and Mobility

In Chapter 2, we learned that the marginal incentive is 1 minus the tax rate. In other words, the amount that you get to keep from the next dollar of income you earn. It is the amount of increase in the marginal incentive that determines the size and impact of a tax cut, even though tax cuts are talked about in terms of the amount of rate reduction.

This may appear to be a technicality, so let's look at an example. Let's say you have two marginal-rate tax cuts, both of ten percentage points. Would you expect them to have the same economic impact? It depends. If a 70 percent tax rate is cut by ten points to 60 percent, then the marginal incentive increases from 30 cents to 40 cents, or one-third. That will have much more impact than a 20 percent tax that gets cut by the same ten points to 10 percent. In that case, you go from keeping 80 cents to 90 cents, which is an increase of 12.5 percent. Size matters, but the size of the change in marginal incentive is more important than the size of the rate reduction.

The Harding-Coolidge tax cuts that shaped the Roaring Twenties reduced marginal tax rates to 25 percent from their prior peak in 1918 of 77 percent. That means people in the top tax bracket kept 75 cents on each additional dollar they earned instead of 23 cents, an increase in the marginal incentive of 226 percent!

People work and invest not to pay taxes but for after-tax income. They can change not only how much they work but when they work, when they invest, and when they spend. An announcement of lower tax rates in the future will reduce taxable economic activity in the present because economic actors shift activity out of the higher-taxed period into the lower. Why earn now and pay higher taxes on the money when you can wait, earn income later, and pay lower taxes on it?

When you evaluate the impact of a phased-in tax cut, it is important to start the measurement period once it has been fully phased in. Those who want to distort the impact of Reagan's tax cuts, which were phased in over a three-year period, often begin the measurement when he took office as opposed to when his policies took effect. The result of postponing economic activity was a sharp recession. The tax cuts didn't ignite the Reagan boom until late 1982.

Capital is extremely mobile, so tax cuts on capital will provoke a stronger response than tax cuts on labor. Moreover, to the extent that capital is double-taxed, which it is in this country, we can expect it to be even more sensitive to tax changes.

Since production drives the economy, we should tax it as lightly as possible, or at most the same as consumption. Therefore, double taxation on production is worse. And worst of all is when you double-tax production and the ones paying the tax also control when the income is realized. That means they control if and when to pay the tax. If the government does anything important, why rely on an undependable revenue stream like this?

For this reason, the correct tax on capital gains (which we explain later is really triple taxation) and repatriated profits (currently double-taxed) should be zero.

Because of their special nature, capital gains will be looked at separately in this chapter.

Over the last century, there have been three major income tax cuts: the Harding-Coolidge cuts in the 1920s, the Kennedy cuts of the 1960s, and the Reagan cuts of the 1980s. Each of these was successful by virtually any metric you want to apply.

The Harding-Coolidge Tax Cuts

The progressive income tax was introduced in 1913 with a top rate of 7 percent. Thanks in part to World War I and the Progressive movement, this tax rate quickly approached 77 percent in 1918. Through a series of reductions, this rate was lowered to 25 percent by 1925.

A look at the difference in key economic metrics four years before the tax cuts and four years after full implementation of the tax cuts reveals the following interesting and instructive picture:

- Federal revenue growth: declined before the cuts at an

average annual rate of 9.2 percent and grew after the cuts at the rate of 0.1 percent

- Real GDP growth: 2.0 percent before the cuts and 3.4 percent after

- Unemployment rate: 6.5 percent before and 3.1 percent after

Although tax rates were cut the most on the highest marginal rates, as they should be, taxes paid by those in the highest brackets doubled as a share of GDP from 30 percent to 62 percent. If you insist on soaking the rich, this is clearly the best way to do it.

With greater capital formation, there was a technological boom. The supply of ideas for making people better off is virtually limitless, so the constraining factor is the amount of capital to finance those ideas. Prosperity is inversely proportional to the wall that separates those with ideas from those with capital. The concept of capital formation sounds complicated. Jack Kemp, a dearly beloved source of inspiration to me and my coauthor, understood the concept as well as anyone. In honor of former congressman Kemp, it is worth repeating. So here goes:

Capital forms when after-tax earnings are not spent and are put at risk. Simple. That's all there is to it. Now you understand capital formation. After you produce, you get paid, you pay taxes, and then you consume. What is left over is available to save or invest. If it is saved, it becomes bank deposits and expands loan capacity for entrepreneurs who want to borrow money in order to grow. If it is invested, it increases the pool of capital and lowers the cost of capital. Thus lower marginal tax rates increase capital formation (as would a cut in the capital gains tax itself, which releases capital presently locked into subpar investments). The result is more growth and innovation and rising living standards.

This is clearly illustrated in the increase in living standards. The Roaring Twenties got their name for a reason. From 1920 to 1930, the percentage of Americans owning an automobile increased from 26 percent to 60 percent. Ownership of home radios increased from 0 percent to 46 percent. Those having electric lighting rose from 35 percent to 68 percent. Those having washing machines rose from 8 percent to 24 percent. Ownership of vacuum cleaners went from 9 percent to 30 percent. And those with indoor toilets increased from 20 percent to 51 percent.[5]

By the end of the decade, the middle class enjoyed many of the items that had been owned only by the very rich at the beginning of the decade. This is what it is all about!

But didn't the "greed" of the Roaring Twenties lead to stock market speculation that caused the crash of 1929? No! Nonsense! This is the narrative that was developed as a rationale to justify massive government intervention. The period was about increased production and living standards. If some people, or even a lot of people, recklessly speculate, the market will dish them losses in due course. That is hardly a reason to take down the whole economy.

What caused the crash is not a simple subject. But in basic terms, the stock market crashed the day after it became apparent the Smoot-Hawley Tariff Act would have enough votes to pass. It was the initial spark, and bad monetary policy by the Fed was the oily rag that turned the spark into a fire. The tax and regulatory policies of Hoover and, later, Roosevelt were the accelerants.[6] For more on the Great Depression, please see section 2 of the FAQs in Chapter 7.

The Kennedy Tax Cuts

From the low of 25 percent during the Coolidge years, top marginal tax rates climbed to an astonishing 94 percent in 1944. How could the economy grow at all with these extraordinarily high tax rates? For one, the capital gains tax was much lower, so some ideas still got financed. But the high tax rates prevented new capital from forming. The rate stood at 90 percent at the start of Kennedy's presidency. Kennedy was a pro-growth supply-sider, which is why Ronald Reagan, Arthur Laffer, Bob Bennett, Jack Kemp, and others were Democrats at that time. In fact, when Kennedy campaigned and won on a platform of low taxes, strong national defense, sound money, and free trade, Democrats controlled all seven major levers of power: the presidency, the U.S. Senate, the House of Representatives, a majority of state governorships, a majority of state legislatures, a majority of Supreme Court appointees, and a majority of Federal Reserve appointees.

In his 1963 Economic Report, Kennedy stated:

> *Tax reduction thus sets off a process that can bring gains for everyone, gains won by marshaling resources that would otherwise stand idle—workers without jobs and farm and factory capacity without markets. Yet many taxpayers seem prepared to deny the nation the fruits of tax reduction because they question the financial soundness of reducing taxes when the federal budget is already in deficit. Let me make clear why, in today's economy, fiscal prudence and responsibility call for tax reduction—even if it temporarily enlarges the federal deficit—why reducing taxes is the best way open to us to increase revenues.*

He later stated in an address to Congress on January 24, 1963:

> *In short, this tax program will increase our wealth far more than it increases our public debt. The actual burden of that debt—as measured in relation to our total output—will decline. To continue to increase our debt as a result of inadequate earnings is a sign of weakness. But to borrow prudently in order to invest in a tax revision that will greatly increase our earning power can be a source of strength.*

The 1964 tax cut (passed after Kennedy's death) cut the top marginal rate from 91 percent to 70 percent by 1965. The cuts had a positive impact on federal revenues, all government revenues, real GDP growth, and unemployment. Comparing the four years before and the four years after the cut, we find the following results:

- Federal revenue growth increased from 2.1 percent to 8.6 percent.

- Combined government revenue (federal, state, and local)

growth increased from 2.6 percent to 9.0 percent.

- Real GDP growth averaged 4.6 percent before and 5.1 percent after.

- Unemployment averaged 5.8 percent before and 3.9 percent after.

One year after the tax cuts, personal income tax revenue exceeded forecasts, particularly among the highest income brackets. Overall, actual receipts exceeded the budget forecast by 36 percent. But in the top income bracket, actual collections beat projections by 80 percent.[7]

Did it work? The tax cut was projected in static terms to reduce federal revenues by $12 billion, but it actually resulted in a $3 billion surplus.

The Reagan Tax Cuts

The Kemp-Roth tax cuts dropped the highest marginal tax rates by 25 percentage points (in three phases), dropped the highest marginal tax rate on unearned income from 70 percent to 50 percent, and immediately cut the capital gains tax to 20 percent.

Because the tax cut was phased in, those who were able to defer economic activity until the lower rates were fully in effect did so. The result was a steepening of the recession that the tax cut was designed to end. But by January 1, 1983, the majority of the tax cuts were implemented, and the results began to show. Comparing the results four years before the 1983 implementation and the four years after show the following:

- Federal revenue reversed: it had been declining at 2.8 percent per year; it was now growing 2.7 percent per year.

- Total government revenue reversed: it was declining at a 2.6

percent annual rate in the four years before the cut; it grew 3.5 percent in the four years after.

- Real GDP growth averaged 0.9 percent before the tax cut and grew 4.8 percent after.

- The unemployment rate increased slightly, from 7.6 percent to 7.8 percent, but that covers up the huge expansion in both the number of jobs created and the size of the labor force. In the four years before the tax cut, employment grew by just 1.2 percent. In the four years after, jobs increased by 11.9 percent.

Beginning with the Steiger-Hansen capital gains tax reduction from 50 percent to 28 percent in 1978, and continuing through the Reagan tax cuts, investment funding boomed. During this period, promising technology companies such as Apple Computer and Microsoft launched initial public offerings of stock, while others such as Cisco Systems and Compaq (later acquired by Hewlett-Packard) received expansion capital and later went public. Furthermore, the telecommunications sector was deregulated, giving us competitive services, cable television, and the advent of wireless communications.

The Clinton Economic Record

It is important to look for a moment at the Clinton economic record. We frequently hear from those selling tax hikes that Clinton raised taxes, and yet we had good growth and a budget surplus in the 1990s, so Clinton's policies had to be good. Therefore, the argument goes, we should raise taxes now if we want a strong economy.

Have you heard that before? The Clinton record offers the best proof that economics trumps politics or party affiliation. Mixing Clinton's entire record into one composite assumes he followed the same policy mix his entire tenure. But the tax policies in his second term far exceeded the economic performance in his first term. It was the same administration. What was the difference?

Part of Clinton's political brilliance was on display when he made a pivot in response to the voters' repudiation of the first two years of his first term. This policy difference can be seen vividly in the nonpartisan S&P 500 index shown in Figure 3-1. Notice what happened right after the 1994 midterm elections.

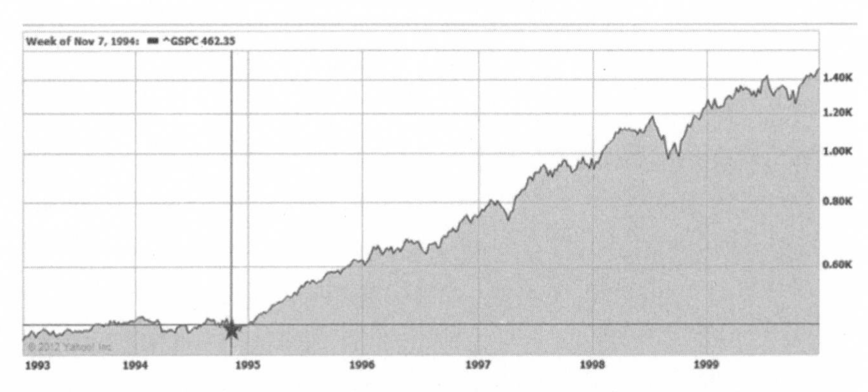

Figure 3-1. S&P 500 Index takes off at the time of the November 1994 election. Source: Yahoo.com

In his first term, Clinton raised taxes and attempted a hostile takeover of the health-care industry. I tried to explain to him at a town hall meeting why it wasn't a good idea, but he didn't listen to me, at least not at the time. But when voters rejected this agenda in epic numbers, he got the message.

As a result of the midterm elections in 1994, Clinton lost fifty-two seats in the House of Representatives and eight more in the Senate, breaking forty years of strong Democratic control. This represented a major political shift—not just a normal midterm election loss for the president's party.

Clinton entered office as a moderate governor who campaigned on middle-class tax cuts, but he clearly telegraphed a tax hike on top income earners and beat an incumbent president who broke his "read my lips, no new taxes" pledge. Despite not having a mandate in terms of the popular vote, he signed into law a large tax increase that, in addition to not receiving a single Republican vote, was opposed by six Democratic senators and forty-one Democratic congressmen.

In 1992, the economy was pulling out of a recession. GDP growth for the entire year was fairly robust. The tax increase slowed the economy some, as would be expected. Economic actors who had the ability to pull income into 1992 and defer expenses until 1993 did so. The distortions can be seen in Figure 3-2, which shows growth slowing from 4.3 percent to an average of 2.7 percent over the next four quarters.

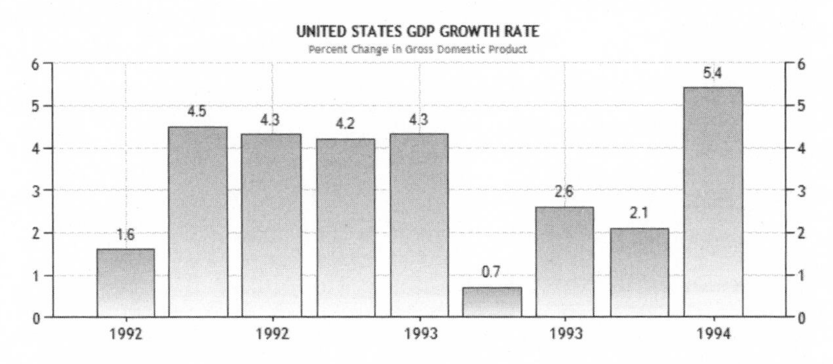

Figure 3-2. GDP growth rate by quarter, 1992–1994. Source: www.tradingeconomics.com, Bureau of Economic Analysis

Personal income growth followed a similar path, growing 6.27 percent in 1992, slowing modestly to 4.14 percent in 1993, and resuming stronger growth of 5.15 percent in 1994.

According to Martin Feldstein, a Harvard professor and former chairman of the Council of Economic Advisers:

Because taxpayers responded to the sharply higher marginal tax rates by reducing their taxable incomes, the Treasury lost two-thirds of the extra revenue that would have been collected if taxpayers had not changed their behavior. Moreover, while the Treasury gained less than $6 billion in additional personal income tax revenue, the distortions to taxpayers' behavior depressed their real income by nearly $25 billion.[8]

Daniel Feenberg of the National Bureau of Economic Research (NBER) joined Feldstein in studying the IRS data from 1992 and 1993. Feenberg and Feldstein concluded that high-income taxpayers reported 8.5 percent less taxable income in 1993 than they would have if their tax rates had not increased. This reduced their additional tax liabilities to less than one-third of what they would have been if they had not changed their behavior in response to the higher tax rates.[9]

They note further that the response to the 1993 increase would probably have been even stronger if taxpayers had had more time to plan. While the tax increase was telegraphed ahead of time, giving many a signal to take certain actions (for example, exercise stock options before the rate went up), the tax hike was passed in August 1993 but made retroactive to January 1, 1993, leaving no time to plan for those wanting to wait for the specifics of the bill.

Not surprisingly, the actual behavior of taxpayers, which seems logical in terms of behavior, is typically at odds with the static thinking of the forecasters on the Joint Economic Committee. This caused the revenue estimators at the Treasury to miss the mark as well. The actual revenue loss was ten times as large as the Treasury staff assumed it would be.

How undeniable is this for those who have actually studied it? Even Austan Goolsbee, President Obama's former economic adviser, concluded that "data confirm that the higher marginal rates of 1993 led to a significant decline in taxable income."[10]

While the economy is most sensitive to changes in marginal rates, Clinton's tax hike included increases on other taxes that were not marginal, and therefore increased revenue without the same distortions to economic activity. Notably, the 1993 action increased taxes on Social Security recipients, subjected personal exemptions to a phaseout, and placed limits on itemized deductions. This increased effective tax rates but not marginal rates. These do a relatively better job generating revenues for the Treasury with less distortion than changes in marginal rates, but this pushes the tax burden down the income ladder.

As details of his tax package became known, Clinton's approval rating hit a low of 37 percent in June 1993, according to the Gallup poll. On the heels of its purely partisan passage, he went after the health-care sector. This focus lasted only from his initial rollout speech in the gallery of the House of Representatives on September 22, 1993, until the end of that year. By the spring of 1994, Republicans were already anticipating sizable midterm gains.

One area where President Clinton deserves strong praise is his embrace of free trade. He passed NAFTA through a Democrat-controlled House, and it went into effect on January 1, 1994. This provided an economic boost to offset some of the negative impact of the tax increase. But the economic boost for the rest of the decade came from tax cuts in 1997, well into his second term.

A note on free trade: As we learned in Chapter 2, all voluntary trade is by definition mutually beneficial. (Government is the only economic actor that can exchange by coercion.) We thus seek to maximize GDP, knowing that it measures how much better off we are. It doesn't matter whether we exchange goods and services across the street, the state, the country, or the world. In the case of free trade, the opening of markets can in no way be considered bad.

But free trade may expose how our tax code mistreats our own domestic producers as compared with producers in the rest of the world. It is not the opening of a foreign market that is bad—it is the tax bias against our U.S. exports. This is the fault of our tax code, not free trade. As part of bilateral free trade, we open our U.S. markets to foreign goods. Because voluntary trade is by definition mutually beneficial, opening up our markets is good. But when we bring in imports, that exposes another bias in the tax code, which favors foreign goods over domestic goods. Again, it is not free trade that is bad, but the unlevel playing field caused by the tax code. In Chapter 4, we will see how 9-9-9 eliminates this bias.

Back to President Clinton. A side effect of his tax increase was an inflation scare that caused the worst bond market in seventy-five years. Inflation, according to Nobel Prize–winning economist Milton Friedman, is too much money chasing too few goods, or an increase in the ratio of money to output. All of us know what inflation means: it takes more money to purchase the same goods. In this case, higher taxes reduced output, and without a commensurate reduction in the money supply, sensitive indicators of incipient inflation caused the Federal Reserve to raise interest rates and thus constrain the larger amount of money chasing goods. During this period, the Fed began to react to the 1993 tax hike and resulting inflation dangers by increasing interest rates rather aggressively, after having consistently eased rates for several years prior to that time. Thus, the tax increase indirectly caused the worst bond market in seventy-five years.

But in the 1994 elections, Republicans picked up fifty-two seats in the House. The stock market started moving and didn't look back, sensing that tax cuts and spending restraint were around the corner. And as Figure 3-1 showed, this was indeed the case.

I do give Clinton credit for restraining spending even while he had a Democratic House. The deficit as a share of GDP began to fall in 1993 and continued this trend through 2000 (Fig. 3-3).

Notwithstanding the hit to GDP caused by the 1993 tax increase,

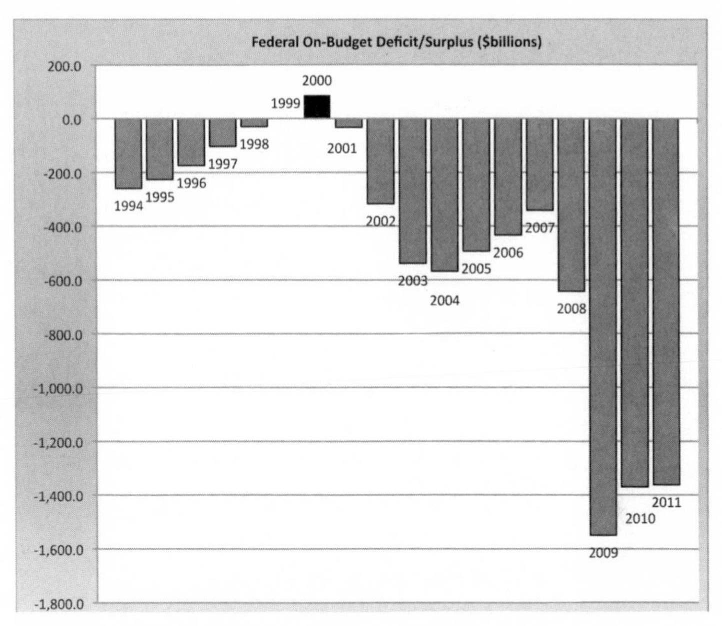

Figure 3-3. Federal deficit, 1994 to 2011. Source: CBO.gov, Revenues, Outlays, Deficits, Surpluses, and Debt Held by the Public Since 1972. On budget deficit/surplus.

spending was fairly restrained each year under Clinton. Outlays grew at an average of "only" 2.8 percent from 1993 to 1999.

With the passage of the capital gains tax cut in 1997, economic growth accelerated, even though we were already six years into the economic recovery. According to J. D. Foster, a senior fellow at the Heritage Foundation, average real GDP growth was 3.2 percent after the tax increase of 1993, but it was 4.2 percent after the tax cut of 1997. Real wage growth averaged 6.5 percent over the four years after the tax cut, compared with a negligible average wage growth of 0.8 percent over the four years after the tax increase.

The tax cut fueled a boom in venture capital funding, according to PricewaterhouseCoopers. By reducing the wall separating people with ideas from people with capital, it allowed more ideas to get financed. In the first full year after the tax cut, funding tripled in comparison with the 1995 level, and by 1999 it had doubled again. This led to the technology revolution all of us know about—one of the greatest revolutions of modern times and a huge contributor to the nation's future.

As expected, realization of capital gains boomed, even with the lower rate. Capital gains tax liabilities averaged $39 billion in the six years prior to the cut in the rate and soared to an average of $103 billion in the four years after.

The budget was in surplus for two years (see Fig. 3-3), a commendable accomplishment that was achieved through spending restraint and strong economic growth driven by lower taxes, monetary stability, and free trade. In 1999, the on-budget surplus (excluding transfers from the Social Security surplus) was only $1.9 billion, making it barely visible on the chart. Subtract the extra capital gains realizations, and it is clear we would not have reached a surplus. In 2000, the on-budget surplus reached $86 billion. That year, tax revenue from capital gains realizations was $131 billion, or $92 billion more than the average before the capital gains tax cut. So those extra capital gains tax revenues accounted for the entire surplus and then some!

Reinforcing this picture, the tax-cut-fueled stock market boom drove an increase in taxes paid on the exercise of stock options. (Note: Clinton inadvertently caused an explosion of executive compensation because contained in his tax hike of 1993 was a provision that prohibited companies from deducting executive compensation in excess of $1 million unless it was related to performance—not for movie stars or professional athletes, but only for executives of publicly traded companies. Of course there was a loophole exempting stock options. This official sanction of stock options made it the compensation of choice for companies. Since then, executive compensation has skyrocketed.)

The IRS does not break out taxes paid on the exercise of stock options. Although such income is directly related to stock market performance, it is considered by the IRS to be ordinary income, not capital income. But as Austan Goolsbee notes:

The data show three things about the relationship between ordinary income and capital income. First, . . . rising stock prices lead to greater option exercise. While intuitive, because most stock option gains are treated as ordinary income, this creates a direct connection between stock market gains and ordinary income and the magnitude is large. Second, capital income is known to be especially sensitive to short-run and expected changes to tax policy. The data . . . show that because of the presence of options, ordinary income of executives was extremely sensitive to anticipated rate changes in the early 1990s, particularly for high-tech executives. Third, there is a direct connection between capital gains tax rates and ordinary income. Falling capital gains rates in 1997 increased the probability of exercising options early to get future stock gains treated as capital gains, again especially for "new" economy executives.[11]

So if you took away the extra revenues from capital gains realizations because of the lower rate and the exercise of stock options, Clinton's famous surplus would not have existed.

The Clinton economic record can be broken down into two segments, one characterized by bad economic policy and one characterized by good economic policy. He came into office against a backdrop of solid economic growth during 1992. The country enjoyed the "peace dividend" that followed the collapse of communism, which aided spending restraint. We had general price stability dating to the mid-1980s. And Clinton helped things by passing NAFTA. Both Democrats and Republicans, however, stopped short of the necessary tax code reforms that would have eliminated the bias against American-made goods and the full benefits of free trade that still elude us.

His tax increase of 1993 caused growth to slow, and the record of income growth in the four years after the tax hike is rather poor, increasing only 5 cents per hour. To his credit, he sensed the political shift of 1994 and made corresponding policy shifts as well. Under his administration, spending restraint was better than under any president of the twentieth century. Whether one assigns credit to him or to Speaker Newt Gingrich—or both—it happened. The crown jewel of his economic policy was the capital gains cut in 1997, which caused acceleration in economic growth six years into the expansion and fueled a venture capital boom that drove the technology boom—a boom that underwrote many of the technological conveniences we accept as standard today.

But without the capital gains tax cut, there would have been no surplus. Economic growth was stronger following the cut. Real wages increased 49 cents per hour in the four years after the tax cut compared with increasing only a nickel per hour in the four years after the tax increase.

The Clinton record is one of the best illustrations that the differences are not about Republicans versus Democrats. They're about good economics versus bad economics. The economy and the stock market are nonpartisan. They respond positively to good policies, whether it's two presidents representing different parties, as in the case of Reagan and Kennedy, or the same president changing from bad policy to good. The same would apply to George W. Bush, who followed poor policy in 2001 and 2008 but sound policy in 2003, which resulted in the best economic period of his presidency.

Capital Gains Taxes

Capital gains are perhaps most sensitive to tax rate changes for several reasons.

1. Capital is mobile and can more easily change location in response to changes in after-tax rates of return.

2. Capital gains are already overtaxed. Taxes are paid once when money is earned and again when after-tax earnings are invested and a gain is realized. I argue they're taxed three times because capital assets increase in value when the present value of expected future after-tax cash flows increase, a third tax.

3. Timing is at the discretion of the holder. You don't pay a

capital gain tax until you decide to realize the gain, so you can avoid paying capital gains taxes indefinitely by not realizing your gains. That's why people tend to take their gains when capital gains tax rates are low, which explains why the Treasury collects more capital gains taxes when there is a lower rate.

Has it always worked this way? Looking at the most recent changes in the capital gains rate, we see the following:

- Kennedy reduced the top capital gains rate, and capital gains revenues increased.

- The 1978 Steiger-Hansen capital gains tax cut increased capital gains revenues after it passed.

- The 1981 cut from 28 percent to 20 percent increased revenues by 50 percent.

- The increase in the capital gains tax rate from 20 percent to 28 percent in 1986 led to a surge in revenues before the increase took effect. Before the increase, realizations almost doubled, to $328 billion, but fell sharply in every year afterward, bottoming out at $112 billion in 1991.

In 1996, the year before President Clinton's capital gains tax cut, capital gains realizations were $261 billion, and capital gains tax revenues were $66 billion.

- In the three years following Clinton's tax cut, capital gains realizations increased $1.37 trillion (compared with the 1996 government forecast of $648 billion).

- Capital gains tax collections exceeded forecasts over the same period by $280 billion versus an expected $195 billion.

- Over the full four years post-cut, total realizations exceeded $2 trillion, and tax collections exceeded $400 billion. (When these were coupled with income from stock option exercising—that is, non-withheld income—along with reasonable restraint in spending growth, the budget hit a surplus.)

During this investment boom, we saw the growth of the Internet, wireless communications, and computing, all key elements of America's economic strength and future.

State Tax Changes

People can change the location of their income. If you don't like the tax policies in the state where you live, you can move to a different one. This explains much of the difference in economic performance among the states and between countries.

Picture two identical companies, A and B, that produce a similar product, draw from the same labor pool, and purchase from the same suppliers—but are separated by an invisible line called a state border.

What happens when taxes go up in company A's state and are reduced in company B's state? Profits decline for A and increase for B. With lower after-tax cash flow, company A faces a declining stock price and a higher cost of capital. (The union pension funds demand satisfactory returns on their portfolio just as much as all investors.) To restore profitability, it must either reduce prices paid to suppliers, reduce wages to employees, or increase prices to customers. In every case, there will be a response. If suppliers lower prices, profits of company A will be restored, but company B will also benefit and maintain a profit advantage that it can use to gain greater market share. If company A reduces wages, it will lose talent to company B. It if raises prices, it will lose market share to company B.

A state's competitive position matters, and after-tax returns are a major factor. In *Rich States, Poor States*, authors Arthur Laffer, Stephen

Moore, and Jonathan Williams compare the economic performance of states that have attractive business environments with that of states that have the least attractive business climates.[12] Of the fifteen factors they use to determine business climate, nine have to do with taxes, three with labor restrictions, two with the size of government, and one with the legal environment. Taxes aren't the only factor—just the dominant one. The results are not surprising, as we see in Table 3-1.

Table 3-1
Comparison of the 10 States That Have the Best Business Climate with the 10 States That Have the Worst Business Climate Versus the U.S. Average

	Top 10 States	**Bottom 10 States**	**U.S. Average**
Gross state product growth	58.5 %	41.6 %	47.0 %
Personal income growth	54.5 %	39.9 %	46.2 %
Personal income growth per capita	44.3 %	41.2 %	41.1 %
Population growth	12.1 %	4.5 %	8.6 %
Net domestic in-migration as % of population	3.0 %	2.40%	0.9 %
Nonfarm payroll employment growth	6.5 %	0.90%	1.5 %
2010 unemployment rate	7.9 %	9.2 %	8.8 %

Source: Arthur B. Laffer, Stephen Moore, and Jonathan Williams, "ALEC-Laffer State Economic Competitiveness Index," in Rich States, Poor States, 4th ed. (Washington, D.C.: American Legislative Exchange Council, 2011).

International Tax Cuts

Interestingly, former communist countries have learned from us and have been heading in the right direction by adopting flat taxes. These increase the tax base, lower the rate, and improve efficiency. They are simple and lighten the burden on production. All of these principles you know by now. Because economics is above politics—even the politics of former communist countries—the results have been quite good.

- In 1994, Estonia became the first country in Europe to adopt a flat tax, of 26 percent. This dramatically reversed its poor economy and enabled it to enjoy sustained growth. Real GDP growth had been declining at 8 percent per year in the five years prior to the implementation of the flat tax; it grew at 4.3 percent in the five years after. Over an eight-year period after its implementation, Estonia's economy sustained growth of 5.4 percent.

- A year later, Latvia followed with a 25 percent flat tax. In the five years before its adoption, Latvia's GDP declined by over half, or minus 11.3 percent per year. In the five years after, its economy grew at 3.8 percent per year.

- Lithuania introduced a 33 percent flat tax in 1994 and experienced similar results.

- And in 2001, Russia implemented a 13 percent personal flat tax, followed by a 24 percent business tax in 2002. In the five years prior to the adoption of these policies, Russia's GDP grew at 1.1 percent, compared with 4.7 percent for the five years after.

These countries learned well what too many American politicians have forgotten—or never understood in the first place. Low tax rates, smartly implemented, lead to widespread prosperity that benefits the people and provides the government with plenty of revenue to fund its operations.

If the members of America's political class are more interested in their own power than in the prosperity that comes from these smart policies, it's time they heard from an Army of Davids.

Chapter 4

The 9-9-9 Plan: Tax Code Replacement

> *If 10 percent is good enough for God Almighty, then 9 percent is good enough for the government.*
>
> *—Herman Cain*

Ronald Reagan was right. There are no easy answers. But there are simple answers. And often, simplicity itself is the answer, because the problem is the result of things getting too darn complicated.

That is the case with our current tax code. It is a mess—different rates, loopholes, deductions, and exemptions, all designed to favor certain entities and certain activities over others. It kills investment, kills growth, and kills prosperity. It needs to be pulled up by the roots and thrown out—replaced by a new code that is simple and fair and treats everyone and everything equally.

That's what 9-9-9 does.

In Chapter 2, we talked about the three stages representing the flow of goods and services in the economy (see Fig. 2-1):

1. Businesses produce goods and services.

2. The income from that production flows to the factors of production (that is, workers and shareholders).

3. That income is used to consume goods and services, meaning that money flows back to businesses, thus completing the circular flow.

To achieve the largest possible tax base, and therefore the lowest possible rate, 9-9-9 taxes all three tax bases equally: production, income, and consumption. This allows us to tax everything once and nothing twice and thus achieve complete neutrality. It is not possible to achieve a larger tax base than this, unless some form of double taxation is introduced.

At this point, some may wonder whether this is triple taxation since we are essentially taxing GDP three times.

It's not triple taxation, because the three tax bases are completely different and the activity being taxed is different. With the incidence of taxation split in this fashion, there will be the fewest opportunities to avoid the tax and the least incentive to do so. This is the key to taxing the widest base possible; this is what allows you to keep rates low and keep neutrality in the code and yet still raise the essential taxes we need.

Once you have determined your base—what activity you will tax; how, where, and who is being taxed—it's easy to determine the tax rate. You simply identify the taxes you will eliminate and replace with 9-9-9, then add up the revenue those taxes raised and do the math of dividing those revenues by the tax base.

The starting point for each tax base is GDP. If tax revenues generally bring between 16 percent and 18 percent of GDP, then one would assume we could just tax everything that makes up GDP at a rate of 16 to 18 percent and be done with it.

But you can't tax all of GDP. Part of GDP is government spending (a part that's growing way too fast), and you can't tax that. Also, certain components of GDP are not the result of private-sector transactions, making them difficult to tax. For example, one component of GDP estimates the "imputed rent of owner-occupied housing." We can't tax that efficiently, so we shouldn't. There are several more of these "imputations," or adjustments, that must be made to the tax bases. You can see more about all this at my website, www.cainfoundations.com, under Scoring Report and Scoring Tables.

So the key is to take those parts of GDP that you can and should tax, and tax them with as much simplicity, transparency, fairness, efficiency, and neutrality as possible. That's what 9-9-9 does.

The 9 Percent Business Flat Tax

Under the first 9, the business flat tax, we want to tax the production of goods and services equally among all businesses. This is a major step forward in tax reform. At present, corporations are taxed differently from partnerships and S corporations; the former pay corporate income tax, while the latter pay taxes through personal income tax returns. The current corporate income tax has become somewhat of a tax haven for the largest corporations, which means the rest must pay a higher rate to make up for it. Instead, we should have one business tax.

Consider, for example, that thirty major companies collectively earned $163 billion of profit, paid $475 million to lobbyists, and paid zero income tax. (See Table 1-2 for a list of the companies.) I don't know whether to be outraged or jealous. Both are bad and counterproductive emotions. I am outraged that you and I are paying for this. I am outraged that small businesses can't compete on a playing field this slanted. I am jealous that I can't pay 0.29 percent of my income to lobbyists to avoid paying 35 percent of my income to the government. And neither can you.

For a given dollar of profits, those big companies provide a dollar in after-tax returns to shareholders. A small business would only deliver

65 cents of that same dollar. This represents a huge cost-of-capital advantage for the biggest companies.

The tax code is responsible for that—by giving big companies tax shelters via the corporate tax that small companies cannot take advantage of. This is a permanent competitive advantage for large corporations, and it is fundamentally wrong!

These big companies are not doing anything illegal. Our current system says it is not. If government says this is the system it wants you to follow, you follow it. In fact, not following it would be wrong. The corporations also have a fiduciary obligation to their shareholders, and it is morally right as a fiduciary to act in the interest of shareholders. It is the system that is completely broken, and tinkering with it won't work. This sucker needs to be ripped out by the roots.

Under 9-9-9, all businesses pay taxes under the same tax system. If the rate gets reduced for one business, it gets reduced for all of them, as it should.

The business tax base is defined as follows:

Business tax base = gross receipts - purchases - net exports - capital investment - labor allowance

Gross Receipts Less Purchases . . .

By taxing gross receipts less purchases, we tax only what the company produces. Purchases from all other businesses are deducted. Why deduct these purchases? Because they represent the cost of goods sold and other overhead expenses, so by not taxing them, we eliminate the compounding of taxes. Those suppliers will pay the business tax too, so all production is taxed only once. To not allow this deduction would be to permit double taxation.

Some have argued that this taxes every stage of production. But how does the current system work? It, too, taxes every stage of production. The farmer's tax is passed to the miller, then on to the baker, the distributor, and the grocer. This system is no different. These are invisible sales taxes, that's all. We reduce them to 9 percent and move the rest to the sales tax, where it is plainly visible.

This is not a new concept. Here is what Calvin Coolidge said in a 1924 address to the National Republican Club in New York:

> *The high prices paid and low prices received on the farm are directly due to our unsound method of taxation. I shall illustrate this by a simple example: A farmer ships a steer to Chicago. His tax, the tax on the railroad transporting the animal, and of the yards where the animal is sold, go into the price of the animal to the packer. The packer's tax goes into the price of the hide to the New England shoe manufacturer. The manufacturer's tax goes into the price to the wholesaler, and the wholesaler's tax goes into the price to the retailer, who in turn adds his tax in the price to the purchaser. So it may be said that if the farmer ultimately wears the shoes he pays everybody's taxes from the farm to his feet. It is for these reasons that high taxes mean a high price level and a high price level in its turn means difficulty in meeting world competition.*
>
> *Most of all, the farmer suffers from the effect of this high price level. In what he buys he meets domestic costs of high taxes and the high price level. It is essential, therefore, for the good of the people as a whole that we pay not so much attention to the tax paid directly by a certain number of taxpayers, but we must devote our efforts to relieving the tax paid indirectly by the whole people.*[13]

As we learned in the Chapter 2, business taxes are invisible sales taxes, and Silent Cal said it as well as anyone. By introducing the national sales tax, we turn invisible sales taxes into visible ones. Taking taxes that are already there and making them visible doesn't increase taxes—or costs, for that matter. It simply increases visibility. (More on the sales tax a bit later.)

. . . Less Net Exports

The deduction of goods purchased by businesses during the production process yields a tax only on that business's production, and thus does not compound the tax. The next step is to deduct net exports; essentially, this means that exports are deducted from the tax base and imports are added to it. This creates what tax reformers have long sought to accomplish but never succeeded: a truly "territorial" tax system. It means that all goods consumed within the United States will be taxed the same way and all goods consumed outside the United States will be taxed the same way according to the country of destination's tax system.

Take a deep breath with me. Ahhhhhh. . . . This ends the tax bias that ships jobs overseas!

I don't know what is worse: a politician who is unaware of one of the most severe economic issues we face or a politician who is aware of it but takes no action. I say they both need to be thrown out of office! This problem has been going on for way too long. It's past time someone did something about it. I served on the board of directors of Whirlpool Corporation, and we faced this difficult situation. You saw earlier how seemingly innocuous differences in tax treatment between large and small companies had a lasting impact on small businesses. The same thing happens internationally, but it is widespread. Before, we were talking about the advantage that thirty companies carved out for themselves. Here, we're talking about a tax bias that affects every single U.S. company—to our country's disadvantage.

Whirlpool's products, which contain the high cost of our tax system in the sales price, are exported all over the world. But they compete with products that don't embed taxes into selling prices, giving Whirlpool's competitors a cost advantage. How? Most export markets have a value-added tax (VAT) that is applied at the retail level. This means goods are manufactured without the tax being embedded in the selling price because the tax is added to the selling price at a later stage. U.S. exports therefore have two taxes: one that gets buried in the price before it leaves the loading dock, and one that gets added at the foreign country's cash register.

Cost structure differences are brutal in competitive markets. They mean Whirlpool doesn't compete as well as it could in world markets. They mean that when the United States negotiates free-trade deals, which it should, sometimes the opening of a new market helps expose this cost differential. It is not the opening of the market that is bad. It is this stupid tax treatment, which is, well, stupid.

Companies can't pass this burden on to shareholders or they will suffer a higher cost of capital, making every future investment more expensive. They can't pass it to consumers, either, or they will lose market share. They can't pass it to employees without reducing their wages. It doesn't leave them with any good options. At Whirlpool, we located facilities outside the United States where we could manufacture goods without embedding our high-cost tax system into the price. This kept us competitive and prevented larger job losses here than we would have had if we had not protected our market share. But look at the convolutions we had to go through to stay competitive—convolutions that not all U.S. companies can duplicate. Why should they have to try? Only a broken tax system punishes its own people, and that's what we've got today.

If you think that's bad, look what this same tax bias does to domestic goods. Imports originate in countries that, for the most part, have a VAT that exempts their exports (which are our imports). Those goods are manufactured without embedded taxes, but instead of having taxes applied at retail, those export goods come here tax-free as our imports. Meanwhile, our domestic goods do have taxes embedded in the selling price. Want to know why imports are so cheap? It's common sense! Our tax code gives tax-free status to imports and taxes the living daylights out of our own domestically manufactured goods.

Who does that help? Certainly not the United States or the American people. No wonder imports make life difficult for domestic manufacturers. Don't blame China. Blame the politicians who have created this monstrosity and stood by while the jobs of their constituents moved overseas.

On a level playing field, we can compete with anyone. It is time to level the playing field so exports compete fairly with world goods and domestic goods compete fairly with imported goods.

This tax adjustment alone will create a huge shift in investment to the United States. Companies will still locate overseas to be closer to end markets, material supplies, and the like. But with this huge tax albatross lifted from around our necks, much more investment will flow here. Once the tax bias is neutralized, it will be easier to see that wage rates in China are more a function of productivity, which is a function of the capital-to-labor ratio (see Chapter 2). If we earn twenty times more per hour, our productivity is twenty times greater because we have more capital invested per worker. A Chinese worker making one-tenth what an American worker makes has a productivity that is one-tenth as large. It is not the wage differentials that are the real problem. It is the tax bias.

Likewise, with a level playing field between imports and domestic goods, demand will shift to domestic goods, and foreign investment will shift to the United States. We will become the capital of capital. What happens to labor when we get more capital investment? You guessed it: more productivity will lead to better wage growth.

In addition, with this structure in place, we can roll out the red carpet and welcome home trillions (yes, trillions with a capital "T") in repatriated profits. These are the profits of U.S. companies that are parked overseas because, if they are brought home, our government would double-tax them. The reason these profits are offshore in the first place is that companies located their businesses outside the United States because of our silly tax laws. When companies locate overseas and earn profits there, they must keep the money there or face double taxation at home. The more profits that build up offshore, the less investment that happens here at home. Jobs follow capital investment, so jobs go abroad. What kind of a system penalizes its own economy and helps its competitors abroad? Why are we letting it rob us of jobs—especially in an economy where unemployment is killing our families and hurting our country?

9-9-9 creates a boundary around the United States and says all goods consumed inside our borders, regardless of whether they originate as domestic or imported goods, will be taxed the same, while all goods for consumption outside the United States will be taxed according to the laws of the country of destination. This makes the tax code fair, efficient, and neutral. If it weren't bad English, I'd say it simply makes it mo' better.

. . . Less Capital Investment

The next deduction is for capital investment. No more depreciation schedules. Full expensing of capital investment. Permanently. If we want wage growth, we need more capital investment. By exempting investment, the business tax becomes the functional equivalent of a consumption tax. If we tax the production of goods minus what is invested, we end up taxing goods that are produced for consumption.

At this point, some people will say that deducting capital investment is unfair to labor. I know you are not thinking that, but someone you talk to might be. So here's the answer. The capital investment occurs with money that has already been taxed. If we start at square one, a business has to make money first in order to invest back into the business. This money has already been taxed once. The idea is to encourage investment in American workers, and to do so, we don't want to double-tax it.

. . . Less Labor Allowance

If we start with gross sales, less purchases, less net exports, less capital investment, we have a 9 percent tax that falls equally on capital and labor and again equally on all businesses. Currently, we have two separate taxes in order to tax capital and labor: namely, the income tax and the payroll tax, respectively. These two separate taxes divide us. We have to fight each other to get tax breaks, which isn't fair to one side or the other. The strong and powerful always end up coming out on top, and the politicians take a cut of the action on both sides. It is total nonsense. It's as if they force us to fight each other, then sell tickets to the fight. We need one tax base that taxes capital and labor the same. That way we have the same incentive to keep rates low. Big business wants to reduce the rate? Great, we all benefit. Big labor wants a lower rate? Fine, we all benefit. Instead of fighting each other, we cooperate with each other. What a concept!

We made an adjustment, however, to the tax that falls to labor, which is a significant upgrade to the current system. Today, businesses pay a 7.625 percent payroll tax for every worker. This starts on the first dollar, has no deductions, and stops at incomes over $106,800. This skews the burden onto people in the lower income brackets. Because this is not fair, it exacerbates the infighting that takes place over taxes. In constructing 9-9-9, we carved out a substantial poverty exemption before determining the 9 percent rate. This means we can exempt from taxation the burden that would fall on the poor. Some of that poverty exemption is applied to businesses to relieve lower-income workers of the burden of the tax on labor. After all, the best way to help the poor is to reduce the government wedge on the lowest incomes. As such, every employer will deduct from the tax base an amount equal to $15,000 per worker. This figure comes from the weighted average of the poverty level as identified by the Census Bureau. As we'll see in the next section covering the personal flat tax, each family takes a poverty deduction that varies according to family size. The business deduction uses an average to treat all workers equally. Besides, my cost to hire you does not depend on the size of your family.

This completely eliminates the tax wedge on the least skilled and least educated workers, who most need relief. Recall that when the tax wedge is reduced, employment and wages increase. This is how you help the poor. The unemployment rate for lower-skilled workers is in sharp contrast to the unemployment rate for the more experienced and better educated. As of December 2011, the unemployment rate was 8.5 percent nationally. But for those with less than a high school diploma, it was 13.8 percent, compared with only 4.1 percent for those with a bachelor's degree and higher.

Among teenagers—the least experienced and least skilled workers—the unemployment rate was 23.1 percent. Among black teens, it was an unconscionable 42.1 percent (compared with 20.3 percent for white teens). This is not a racial issue but a government wedge issue. The government wedge is larger in the inner city because of counterproductive economic policies perpetuated by the so-called progressives who control these cities. Although not part of 9-9-9, my campaign rolled out Opportunity Zones as a way to further attack the government wedge that is holding back our most distressed areas, including many urban and rural areas. For further reading, the policy rolled out by my campaign is posted to the website. In addition, I suggest you read Stuart Butler of the Heritage Foundation. Teens need on-the-job training! First of all, the minimum wage is set higher than the marginal productivity of most of these inexperienced, unskilled workers. That is why they are unemployed! On top of the cost of the minimum wage, the employer has to pay another 7.625 percent payroll tax. Under 9-9-9, there is a zero tax wedge where it is needed the most. It is like paying them cash under the table, but doing it legitimately and on the books.

Under the business flat tax, the 9 percent tax that falls to labor starts at $15,000 rather than the first dollar. Furthermore, it is not capped, so all wages above this level, including that of the CEO, are taxed equally. The cost of hiring a worker (part of the wedge) is lowest at the lowest income levels, where worker productivity is least likely to overcome an additional cost burden, and highest at the highest income levels, where it can most easily be overcome by productivity.

The labor allowance of $15,000 per worker makes the effective tax rate that applies to the labor portion of the business tax a progressive tax. If you must have a progressive tax, it is best to do so with the effective rate rather than the marginal rate. Thus, the effective tax on labor is zero for someone making $15,000, it is 4.5 percent for someone making $30,000, and it is 9 percent for Barbra Streisand and others making millions.

At this point, if we did a blind taste test on 9-9-9 and listed some of the features without saying that it was advanced by a Republican candidate, it would go something like this:

1. Do you favor taxing capital and labor at the same rate?

2. Do you favor shifting the burden of the labor tax away from the lower end of the worker population toward the CEOs?

3. Do you favor closing loopholes and eliminating special-interest deductions?

4. Do you favor ending the tax bias that ships jobs overseas?

5. Do you favor allowing our exports to compete on a level playing field?

6. Do you favor ending the practice of penalizing domestic goods and giving tax-free status to imports?

7. Do you believe that those thirty large U.S. companies that paid lobbyists millions but paid none in taxes should pay the same taxes as all other businesses?

8. Do you favor policies that will attract capital to the United States rather than repel it?

9. Do you believe we should have the most productive workforce in the world?

Not one person in a million would answer no to any of these questions. I don't care whether you are talking about the Tea Party or Occupy Wall Street, good economics trumps bad politics. Uniting is better than dividing. And anytime you can get those two groups agreeing on tax policy, you are onto something good. Do you see why my plan caught on the way it did?

Are you ready to pass 9-9-9 yet? Not so fast, I'm just getting warmed up.

All of the year-end tax-planning guides that fill the shelves each tax season will simply say the following in the business tax section: invest more in your workers or export more.

If you step back for a minute, all we've done is change one single line item on a business's income statement: the tax liability. This severs the link between the calculation of the tax and the calculation of net income. This may take some getting used to. Net income is calculated the same way it has always been calculated, but with one difference: the amount of tax due.

I hope you find this next part as interesting as I think it is. Once net income is determined, it flows over to the personal flat tax. That's right. This, in effect, extends partnership treatment to corporations, another level playing field! Now we can tax capital (shareholders) the way we tax labor (employees) under the personal tax just as we do under the business tax. Don't you just love level playing fields?

From a business standpoint, this eliminates the double taxation of dividends and makes it neutral whether companies pay dividends or retain earnings. Under 9-9-9, business net income is attributed to shareholders regardless of whether dividends are paid.

Let's walk through an example. A company earns $1 per share in after-tax net income. You own 100 shares. If the company retains all of the earnings, it remits your 9 percent tax for you and sends a tax document (like a 1099 or W-2) that says you must pick up $100 of additional earnings, but that 9 percent tax has already been withheld and remitted to the IRS. This doesn't impact your cash flow. The tax has been paid for you. It is a noncash entry on your personal return. If the company pays all of the earnings as a dividend, you receive a check for the full $100. This is a cash transaction, so you pay the tax. If the company does as most companies do and retains some earnings while paying out some as a dividend, the same mechanics work. In a case where $50 is retained as earnings and $50 is paid as a dividend, you get the tax document that instructs you to report the $50 and shows that taxes of $4.50 have been paid; you also receive a dividend check for $50 on which you must pay $4.50 in tax.

By having businesses pay at 9 percent and individuals pay at 9 percent, we integrate both tax systems. This eliminates the gamesmanship of converting one type of income to another in order to try to take advantage of a lower rate—a nonproductive activity that reduces output. This "new" concept has been long desired by tax reformers, going all the way back to the landmark document Blueprints for Basic Tax Reform, published by the Department of the Treasury in 1977. Since then, people have talked about "integration." But don't confuse motion for action. The politicians have not touched this. Why not? Is it possible that perhaps—just perhaps—doing so would screw up a major source of campaign contributions?

The 9 Percent Personal Flat Tax

Income subject to the personal flat tax is defined simply as gross income less charitable deductions and a poverty exemption. The resulting adjusted income is taxed at 9 percent.

Under the personal tax, like the business tax, capital and labor are taxed equally. Recall that business net income flows to the shareholders and is taxed right alongside wages at the same rate. Capital income, or the return on capital, should be taxed the same as labor income.

Capital gains should not be taxed. It is a triple tax on production whose realization is voluntary. To the extent the government does anything important, why would you want to fund it with a revenue source that is voluntary? That's stupid. Get out the firing squad and execute it.

The main reason to eliminate it is that it separates ideas from capital. We want ideas to come to life. The supply of ideas for making people better off is virtually limitless. The real constraining factor is the amount of capital to finance them. By eliminating the capital gains tax, we instantly increase capital formation. Today, capital is often stuck in investments that produce subpar returns because the capital gains tax makes it too costly to move the capital to better investments. The result is that fewer new ideas get financed because capital is locked into old ideas. The result is less growth.

Increased capital formation is the key to making the United States the capital of capital. Doing so will be a strong driver of wages. In addition to unlocking capital gains, the 9 percent marginal tax rate means more new capital will form. If you now keep 91 cents on the next dollar you earn or produce, you have a strong incentive to produce more. You have more with which to save or invest. In fact, compared with the present top marginal rate of 35 percent, you will keep 26 cents more on the dollar (91 - 65 = 26). Since it is a revenue-neutral plan, most of us will be about the same in a static sense. That is, on day one, what you give up in deductions you will get back in the form of a lower tax rate. But on day two, and every day thereafter, you have strong incentives to work and produce and enjoy more of the fruits of your labor on every new, or marginal, dollar you earn or invest.

Businesses will have strong incentives to invest, and individuals will have not only more capital but an equally strong incentive to invest in businesses. This is the type of self-reinforcing positive growth cycle we need to accelerate our way out of this economic mess.

Charitable gifts will be the only deductions that remain and will follow the current requirement that the recipient have 501(c)(3) status. Here is a problem that I readily acknowledge. Private charity under 9-9-

9 is not deductible. If you assist a neighbor down the street who is sick or in need of help by providing meals, running errands, or donating clothing or household items, you don't get a deduction under 9-9-9. But under the current tax system, you don't get a deduction either, so that is not the issue. On that score, nothing changes.

We keep this deduction in place because it's a calculation we've made that now is not the time to eliminate this deduction. Once we become the capital of capital and our economy is booming and wage growth is strong, everyone will realize that prosperity drives charitable giving, not the tax code. In a better economic environment, removing this deduction could be accomplished since the tax break will only have a 9 percent benefit in the first place. But only if the tax rate is reduced commensurate with the elimination of the deduction would I ever consider it.

The mortgage interest deduction is a different matter. It has diminished in value over the years and is not as important as overall economic growth in helping to ease the housing downturn.

When mortgage interest was first given preferential treatment in 1986, average mortgage interest rates were 10 percent and median home values were $92,230. (Interest was always deductible. In 1986 interest deduction was eliminated, but not for mortgages, making it the first time mortgage interest was given preferential treatment.) The interest deduction of $9,223 was 2.5 times the standard deduction of $3,670. Over time, the deduction has lost its impact. Today, the median home price of $147,000 and an average mortgage rate of 4 percent represent only half the standard deduction. Back in the day, if you owned a median-priced home, you automatically itemized your taxes, allowing you to claim additional deductions. It was a real nice deal. Today, that is no longer the case.

Even owning the median-priced home doesn't get you much in the way of deductions. You must have other deductions that are at least as valuable as your mortgage interest just to break even with the value of the standard deduction. Consequently, the benefit has gradually drifted up the income scale, and there is less benefit to those in the lower half of the income scale. Moreover, this deduction, unintentionally of course, limits labor mobility. If your skill set is such that you must relocate to where the jobs are but you can't move because you are a homeowner who can't sell his house, you are not getting much benefit. The economy functions better with more labor mobility. Under 9-9-9, renters will be put on a level playing field with homeowners. Finally, and most important, economic growth is the key to reviving the housing market, case closed.

All families will deduct the poverty level from their taxable income. The published poverty levels vary based on family size, so larger families take a larger deduction. The Census Bureau publishes these figures; see, for example, Table 4-1.

Table 4-1

Poverty Thresholds for 2010 by Size of Family and Number of Related Children Under 18 Years

		Related Children Under 18 Years								
Size of Family Unit	**Weighted Average Thresholds**	**None**	**One**	**Two**	**Three**	**Four**	**Five**	**Six**	**Seven**	**Eight or More**
One person, unrelated adult	11,139									
Under 65 years	11,344	11,344								
65 years and over	10,458	10,458								
Two people	14,218									
Householder under 65 years	14,676	14,602	15,030							
Householder 65 years and over	13,194	13,180	14,973							
Three people	17,374	17,057	17,552	17,568						
Four people	22,314	22,491	22,859	22,113	22,190					
Five People	26,439	27,123	27,518	26,675	26,023	25,625				
Six People	29,897	31,197	31,320	30,675	30,056	29,137	28,591			
Seven People	34,009	35,896	36,120	35,347	34,809	33,805	32,635	31,351		
Eight People	37,934	40,146	40,501	39,772	39,133	38,227	37,076	35,879	35,575	
Nine people or more	45,220	48,293	48,527	47,882	47,451	46,451	45,227	44,120	43,845	42,156

Source: U.S. Census Bureau.

So the 9 percent personal tax starts on the first dollar above the poverty level for all families.

Allow me to dispel some controversy. (The nice thing about writing a book is that I can talk without getting interrupted.) The plan all along was to create a significant exemption for the poor, which we did. We calculated the total exemption amount by multiplying the poverty threshold by the number of families in that size cohort. For example, in Table 4-1, the average poverty level for a four-person family is $22,314. Also using Census Bureau data, we determined that there are fifteen million four-person families. We proceeded to multiply each poverty threshold by the total number of families in the United States that were of the same size. This grand total of the weighted average exemption was then deducted from the tax base before we determined the 9 percent rate.

Under the business tax, giving every business a labor allowance of $15,000 only used one-third of our total poverty exemption. In the personal tax, allowing every family to exempt the poverty level from tax used up only another third. The last third was reserved for geographically designated Opportunity Zones, which were modeled after Jack Kemp's original plan.

Here is where we got attacked. We didn't announce exactly how the poverty exemption was going to be used when we first rolled out the plan. We just said that there will be additional deductions under the business and personal taxes. This is where I should take credit for masterminding a plot to get the media and the "nonpartisan" think tanks to reveal their true colors by setting them up for one giant knee-jerk reaction.

If I actually planned it this way, boy, was it brilliant. Because what happened next was incredible. Reporters, organizations, and others not interested in the facts—only in attacking—exploded with charges of "it will hurt the poor." As my grandma would say to politely dismiss someone who is rudely wrong: "Bless their hearts."

We published the full scoring report and tables in September 2011. They were posted to our website and can now be found at www.cainfoundations.com. On page 4 of the Scoring Tables, viewers will see

Table 6, which is the full calculation mentioned above. We put this out for the world to see and encouraged all to do so. We told everyone to go to our website and get this great new scoring report. I was proud to have been the only presidential candidate to put out a fully detailed and fully scored major tax reform plan. There is no way we were trying to hide this from anyone.

The high point of the knee-jerk reaction came just hours before the Las Vegas debate, when a liberal think tank disguised as "nonpartisan" released a report claiming 9-9-9 hurt 84 percent of Americans. What!? It turns out that the Tax Policy Center is a front group for the liberal Brookings Institution and the Urban Institute. Figure 4-1 is a screen print from its website. Of course the highlighted part is mine.

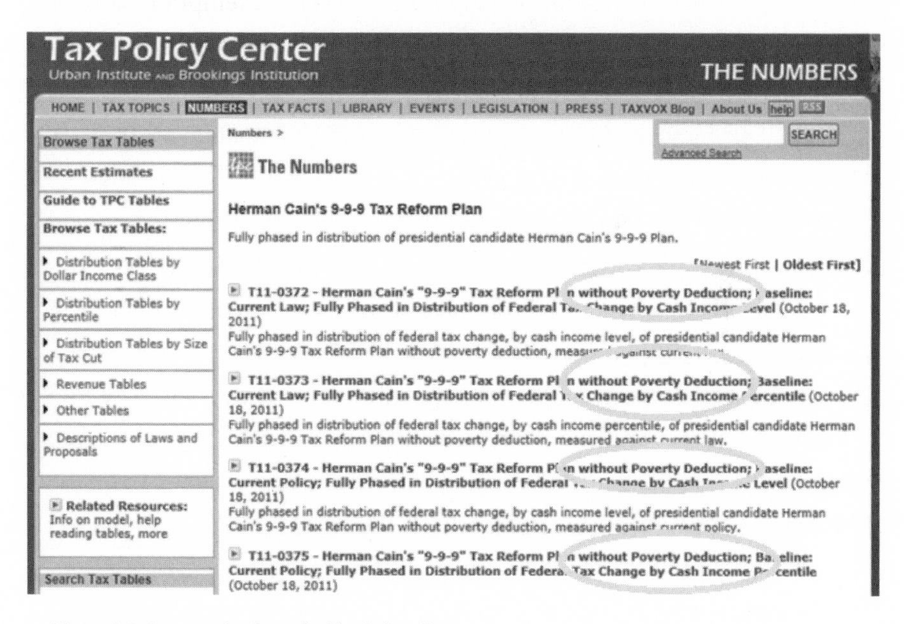

Figure 4-1. Screen print from the Tax Policy Center.

The Tax Policy Center does not hide the fact that it excluded the entire amount of our poverty exemption, which, as you now know, is considerable. We told the people there, and everyone else, that we had a large exemption. We told them, and everyone else, that we would fully use it. The only thing we waited to specify was how exactly it would be applied. To anyone nonpartisan, which the center claims to be, with its staff of "experts," and to all those who claim, according to its own website, that the group "provides timely, accessible analysis and facts about tax policy to policymakers, journalists, citizens, and researchers," I have three short questions. What facts? What experts? What analysis? The only thing timely was a hit job two hours before a debate. How could one totally exclude every penny of a well-publicized poverty exemption merely to draw the unfounded conclusion that we hurt the poor? Oh, by the way, another flaw in the center's report, as if one fatal flaw weren't enough, is the assumption that the sales tax is an add-on tax that increases prices. I doubt the experts at the center will read this book and learn that our sales tax simply replaces other taxes already embedded in the price, but there it is. Out-of-pocket costs, and therefore the burden, do not go up. Only visibility goes up.

Perhaps I pick on the Tax Policy Center a bit too much here, because there are many others who deserve to be singled out and called to account for their own giant knee-jerk reactions, but I will run out of space in this book if I try to do that.

Why didn't we announce all this right up front? We had a purpose for rolling out Opportunity Zones separately. We took them seriously and wanted to do them right. They were too important to combine into one plan. We can't get the distressed areas turned around without first putting the whole country on a strong growth path, which 9-9-9 does. And we can't have genuine prosperity if the whole country is booming but we leave the most distressed areas behind, which we address with Opportunity Zones.

The first statement I made at the rollout of Opportunity Zones was that because we got rid of the capital gains tax and had full expensing of capital investment for the whole country, à la Jack Kemp, the whole country was one giant Opportunity Zone. At that point, we specified the amounts to be taken under the business taxes and personal taxes. Mind you, that still used up only two-thirds of our exemption. The last third was saved for the geographic zones.

All along, we indicated in the 9-9-9 brochures and materials that there were additional deductions under both the business and the personal taxes for Opportunity Zones. (Some early materials still called them Empowerment Zones, but we later changed the name only to distance our plan from the messed-up version passed by President Clinton.)

Besides helping the poor, the plan is friendly to families. Because the poverty level is in relation to family size, there is a larger exemption for larger families. The idea should never be to see how much we can exempt from taxation. That just reduces the tax base, pushing the rate higher than it needs to be. That moves us again in the wrong direction, toward having half the country not paying tax. The goal should be to see how low we can get the rate.

This also eliminates the marriage penalty. If one spouse works, fine: pay 9 percent above poverty. If both work, fine: pay 9 percent above poverty.

With a tax code this simple, the size, scope, and power of the IRS will be greatly reduced. We may only need to retain enough clerks to receive money and transfer it to the Treasury. Gone will be the bullies who create nightmares for millions. No more "guilty until proven innocent" audits. In 1926, the Supreme Court noted that a statute that is "so vague that men of common intelligence must necessarily guess at its meaning and differ as to its application, violates the first essential of due process of law." A simple tax code will restore due process.

Many people will not even have to file a return. The design calls for withholding to start on the first dollar of income. The only information needed to process the refundable poverty exemption is one's family size. There is no reason that couldn't be submitted to the employer ahead of time. That way, following year end, you would not have to file a return—just wait for the refundable exemption. Of course, if you make a charitable contribution or if your family size changes during the year, you would have to file a return to get more money back. But how complicated could such a tax return be? It might have two sections:

> Section A: If your family size changed, indicate the difference, and we'll recalculate your refundable exemption based on the new family size.
>
> Section B: If you made a charitable contribution, fill in the amount, and we'll send you 9 percent of that amount.

The refundable credit means that those below the poverty level still face a 9 percent marginal rate. Below the poverty line, one additional dollar of income will result in 9 percent less refund. Once you get above the line, each dollar of income results in 9 percent being taxed. Either way, it is a 9 percent levy. Maintaining this linear relationship, where the marginal incentive is always 91 percent for everybody, is an important achievement. Too often, programs designed to help the poor create a poverty trap. That is because at some point the benefits get phased out as income rises. If we treat the loss of a benefit as a "tax," since it has the same effect as a tax, then we see that as a poor person works his or her way up, the combination of real taxes and the phaseout of means-tested benefits—which act like taxes—results in a combined "tax" burden of over 70 percent! The highest marginal tax rates are not in the wealthy suburbs. They are in the poorest neighborhoods! Where are the Tax Policy Center, the Washington Post, and CNN covering this? To see this for yourself, go to the National Center for Children in Poverty. Its website is quite helpful, and we used some of its calculators to help form our Opportunity Zones policy.

The 9 Percent National Retail Sales Tax

Tax reformers have long advocated taxing consumption rather than production. And for good reason. It makes sense. But a strong divide has developed on how to get there. Instead of advocating pro-growth tax reform in a united voice against the progressives, we are in a tug-of-war against each other. Flat-tax supporters say a properly structured flat tax that exempts investment is the equivalent of a consumption tax. They are right. Supporters of the FairTax claim their pure form of a consumption tax is better. They are right. The longer this tug-of-war continues, the longer we are sentenced to another year of this terrible tax code.

In the name of uniting the country, uniting all businesses under the same code, uniting all individual taxpayers under the same code, uniting those wanting to eliminate deductions with those wanting to lower rates, and uniting individuals and businesses under the same rate, we must unite the two main camps comprising the base of tax reform supporters. I have had strong indications from supporters of each camp that 9-9-9 is the way to unite both groups. After all, it is a combination of the flat tax and the FairTax. Because both the business tax and the personal tax exempt investment, they are equivalent to a consumption tax. This makes the whole plan the functional equivalent of a consumption tax.

The sales tax base is modeled after the FairTax. We tax final retail sales, which exclude business-to-business sales. There are no deductions or exemptions, so, yes, it applies to food, clothing, and everything else. There is a big difference between this sales tax and the type of sales tax usually found in the states. A state sales tax is an add-on tax that does increase prices. Therefore, because the higher prices make it harder for the poor to afford the same products, the states must exempt basic necessities. This, however, is a replacement tax of taxes already embedded in the cost of products. To illustrate, if all taxes are directed to businesses, and there is no income tax and no sales tax, these taxes will still come out of our pockets. It's just that we won't see the taxes. This lack of visibility feeds a higher tax burden because it reduces the number of people aligned to keep rates low. Now, if all these taxes are shifted to a visible consumption tax, the total cost doesn't change, the total tax doesn't change, and there is no reason for the consumer's out-of-pocket cost to change. The only thing that changes is visibility! With a highly visible tax, now all Americans are united in holding the line on taxes.

Used goods are not subject to the tax in the same way. These goods have already been produced, taxed, and consumed. We are not going to tax them again. However, the markup or sales commission on a used good will be subject to a tax. A house purchased from the existing housing stock would face a sales tax only on the agent's commission, not on the purchase price. But what about new homes? Won't the sales tax hurt new home sales? By now, I bet you are getting the hang of this. You are probably saying, "Herman, I know the answer to this. The price of a new home includes the tax of the lumberyard, the taxes of the builder, the plumber, the painter, the electrician, etc." Exactly right! A new home that sells for $250,000 today under the existing system would sell for more like $225,000, plus the 9 percent sales tax, or right about where we started. How do we know prices will adjust like this? There are two reasons. First, in an economic sense, the marginal cost of production will decline because of the reduction in marginal tax rates. When marginal costs decline, price pressure is downward. To argue otherwise is to argue against gravity. The reason technology prices keep declining is that marginal costs are continually pushed downward and competition drives prices toward marginal costs.

Second, we have enlisted the largest, most established, most effective, most accountable, and most feared enforcement group in the country. They have a strong presence in every state and membership numbers in the hundreds of millions. They are called American consumers.

If you see a product that doesn't pass these savings along, don't buy it. It's common sense. Chances are businesses will be quick to respond. As soon as 9-9-9 legislation is introduced, businesses would be wise to recalculate their costs for products already sitting on the shelves. It would be fairly straightforward for the company to figure out the lower price, which may result in a lower profit initially, but that would be taxed at a lesser rate. A bottle of water costing $1 today would more likely be repriced at 90 cents, and the new sales tax would be applied to that figure. On balance, consumers come out about the same, but we have raised the visibility of the tax. The more visible taxes are, the more we know what government really costs us, the less government we will demand. This is the problem the progressives have with the sales tax. They cloak it in concern for the poor, but the poor will be helped by 9-9-9. They always use the poor to conceal their agenda.

The other advantage of the sales tax is that it helps level the playing field between domestic goods and imports. In the section covering the business tax, we talked about how imports will be subject to the business tax. Imported goods will also bear a share of the sales tax. This means that if you line up a domestic good with an imported good, both will bear 9-9-9, as it should be.

In addition, the consumption tax will capture some of the underground economic activity once that unreported income is spent. This could be from the illegal drug business, illegal immigrants, and so forth. It will shift some of the burden to tourists because the idea is to tax all activity the same within our borders.

Under 9-9-9's design, it is not necessary to issue "prebate checks," which are necessary under the FairTax. The prebate is the FairTaxers' way of exempting the poor. Since they tax only one tax base, they have only one tax base through which to deliver relief to the poor. They have no other choice. We have three choices, and we formulated the best way. First, some of the exemption is used to give every employer a labor exemption of $15,000 per worker. This is common sense. The best way to help someone is with a job. The other portion is given to families directly against income. This is common sense too. This reduces the tax wedge to zero at the poverty level, which should expand employment and wages at the low end.

The Tax Base, Tax Rates, and Revenue Neutrality

We chose 2008 for our baseline to construct the tax tables since that was the last year without significant distortions in the composition of GDP resulting from the Great Recession. The key to a revenue-neutral tax plan is that in a static sense it brings in the same revenue and in a dynamic sense it causes no negative distortion. As you can tell already, there will be significant positives to this plan in a dynamic sense. The economy will boom when we become the capital of capital (and get sound money and a Regulatory Budget Office, but that is getting ahead of ourselves). When we compare the likely state of the economy under 9-9-9 with the current system, it is impossible to use a future year as a basis of comparison because we don't know what a future year's economy will look like. But we get a lot closer by doing the comparison based on a recent tax year for which the numbers are already in the books, so to speak.

With 2008 as the base year, the tax base of the business flat tax was $9,480 billion according to our definition of gross sales, less purchases, less net exports, less capital investment, less a labor allowance of $15,000 per employee.

The tax base of the personal flat tax was defined as gross income, less charitable deductions, less a poverty deduction. The poverty deduction is according to the census figures and varies based on family size. In the aggregate, this base amounted to $7,702 billion of adjusted personal income.

The tax base for the national sales tax was $10,263 billion.

9-9-9 would replace only these taxes: personal and corporate income taxes, both the employer and the employee portion of payroll taxes, the death tax, and the capital gains tax. We do not replace all federal revenues, only those we have found guilty of committing "capital offenses" against the economy and deserving of execution.

In the baseline year of 2008, these taxes generated the following amounts:

Personal income taxes	$1,102.8 billion
Corporate income taxes	200.5 billion
Payroll taxes	972.4 billion
Estate and gift taxes	28.2 billion
Total	$2,303.9 billion

$2,303.9 billion is 16 percent of baseline 2008 GDP.

Note: The alternative minimum tax (AMT), which also merits the death penalty under 9-9-9, and the capital gains tax are not broken out separately, because they are included in the personal income tax figures. The tax on repatriated corporate profits, deserving of execution, is included in the corporate tax above. Several sources of federal revenue remain and are not replaced by 9-9-9. These represented 1.4 percent of GDP, or approximately $200 billion in the baseline year, and include all kinds of miscellaneous things such as excise taxes, custom duties, the Railroad Retirement Investment Trust, and a few others.

Those who assert that 9-9-9 isn't revenue neutral often do so under the false assumption that it replaces all federal taxes, which it doesn't. As a result, their argument is off by about $200 billion. The reason we leave some sources of federal revenue alone is that they are not the worst offenders and have not committed a "capital crime" against the economy. After all, an excise tax is a pretty efficient tax. It taxes consumption, which is good. It taxes only the specific users, which is good. And it doesn't affect marginal rates, to name another positive feature.

Putting it all together, we get this:

Taxes to be replaced	$2,303.9 billion
Tax bases:	
Business	$9,480 billion
Personal	7,702 billion
Consumption	10,263 billion
Less allowance adjustments	-1,992 billion

Total tax bases $25,654 billion

The tax rate is $2,303.9 billion/$25,654 billion = 9 percent.

Note: The amount reserved for adjustments was originally intended to provide additional incentives for geographically designated Opportunity Zones. If the next Congress does not pursue them, I advise using this amount to provide transition allowances as deemed necessary.

The 9-9-9 plan would bring in $2,303.9 billion of revenues in a static sense, equal to the $2,303.9 billion the federal government collected in the base year. But since we would be stimulating the economy big-time—that's what you consider when you do dynamic analysis—our taxes would undoubtedly lead to even more in revenues, making an even greater cut in the deficit and making even lower rates possible.

Dynamic Scoring

9-9-9 was independently scored by Gary Robbins of Fiscal Associates. Mr. Robbins is a former Reagan Treasury official who oversaw that department's econometrics function. He verified the construction of the tax bases, the determination of the tax rates, and the revenue-neutrality calculation. He also conducted a dynamic analysis of 9-9-9's impact on the economy. According to his analysis, 9-9-9 will expand GDP by $2 trillion, increase private-sector business investment by one-third, generate 6 million new jobs, increase wages by 10 percent, and bring in 15 percent more federal revenue—enough to reduce rates a total of 4 more percentage points. So if taxes as a share of GDP are the same, but we raise that much more revenue, that tells you just how much damage politicians do to the economy with all their tinkering and manipulation.

Questions I Have for You

Issues that have yet to be debated will require your input. How do we properly manage the rate structure once it is operational? Because of the strong growth effects, revenues will surely exceed the static revenue-neutral estimate. There are several plausible alternatives to be considered:

1. Apply all additional revenues to reducing the deficit.

2. Apply additional revenues toward lower tax rates to keep feeding economic growth.

3. Do a combination of deficit reduction and further rate cuts.

4. Cut spending to close the deficit, and direct all additional revenues to further rate reductions.

5. When it comes to rate reductions, reduce them evenly to ensure we maintain the same kind of neutrality, heading toward 8-8-8 and then 7-7-7.

6. Reduce the business tax and personal tax only, leaving the consumption tax alone, which is a gradual transition to a FairTax (for example, 7-7-9, then 6-6-9, and so on).

7. Reduce only the business tax, since it is the only tax that is not 100 percent visible (for example, 5-9-9, then 3-9-9).

8. Reduce the personal and business taxes with additional revenues, and gradually shift a percent or 2 at a time from the personal and business taxes over to the consumption tax to arrive at a FairTax faster: for example, 6-6-11, then 3-3-15.

I would like to hear from you. Send your preference to my website, www.cainfoundations.com.

Chapter 5

The Benefits of 9-9-9

Rocket fuel for the economy.

—*Stephen Moore, Wall Street Journal*

"9-9-9" Popularity Soars to Historic Levels

The popularity of 9-9-9 cuts across racial, gender, and geographic lines. In a recent poll, the plan had a 76 percent familiarity with a net positive of 24 percentage points, 50 percent to 24 percent.[14] According to the polling firm Strategic National, "Very few economic plans in the recent hyper-partisan era have had the broad support of so much of the American electorate." While Republicans view the plan favorably by a margin of 65 percent to 15 percent, and independents by a margin of 56 percent to 20 percent, even 33 percent of Democrats rated the plan "very" or "somewhat" favorably.

Importantly, the plan scores well among the fastest-growing racial subgroups of the country. Among Hispanics, support was 62 percent favorable to just 22 percent unfavorable. Figures for Asian respondents were 54 percent favorable to 23 percent unfavorable.

As confirmation of my intent to unite the country, favorability among blacks is not that much different from that among whites. White respondents favored 9-9-9 by a score of 50 percent versus 26 percent unfavorable, while blacks responded 48 percent favorable to 28 percent unfavorable.

My friends, it's catching on. Finally, we have a simple, transparent, efficient, fair, and neutral tax code.

Everywhere I went on the campaign trail, I heard the same comment about 9-9-9: it gets Washington out of the middle of the tax code. No more picking winners and losers. No more special tax breaks for some that cause higher rates for the rest. It treats all of us fairly. 9-9-9 improves transparency because the personal tax and the sales tax are 100 percent transparent and paid by 100 percent of every politician's constituents. It is efficient, raising the same revenue while helping the economy, not harming it. It lifts a massive $431 billion deadweight compliance burden off the back of the economy. It levels playing fields so that capital is taxed the same as labor, small business is taxed the same as large corporations, exports are taxed the same as world goods, imports are taxed the same as domestic goods, and dividends are taxed the same as retained earnings.

9-9-9 Ends the Tax Bias That Ships Jobs Overseas

Businesses don't ship jobs overseas; the tax code does. To fix this, exports are deducted from the business tax. They never see the sales tax. They are liberated to compete with the rest of the world on a completely level playing field. At the margin, this will shift investment to the United States. Imports pay the business tax and a share of the sales tax, which means they pay 9-9-9 just like domestic goods pay 9-9-9.

Leveling this playing field will shift demand to domestic goods and shift more foreign investment here. Repatriated profits, currently trapped overseas because of double taxation, will be welcomed home. There is no reason to treat these profits with hostility. They were driven there by the tax code and trapped there by it too. Whether they are invested to expand output, pay higher dividends, repurchase shares, reduce debt, pay higher wages, or just sit in our banks instead of foreign banks (increasing bank deposits, which increases loan capacity), bringing this capital home to be invested in the United States can do absolutely no harm.

9-9-9 Is the Right Way to Help the Poor

The best way to help the poor is with a strong, vibrant economy that is generating strong job growth and rising wages. 9-9-9 is expected to expand the economy by $2 trillion, create 6 million jobs, and increase wages by 10 percent. That is a good first step. The tax wedge is reduced the most at the lower income levels, reaching zero at the poverty level. Unemployment is highest among the least educated, least skilled, and least experienced workers. This targets relief where it is needed most. Business gets a $15,000 labor allowance per employee, which is more valuable at the lower end of the wage scale and loses value as wages climb. All families get an exemption equal to the poverty level, so effective tax rates are lowest at the lower income levels. This retains a progressive feature, where effective taxes will range from 0 to 9 percent depending on income, but without the damage caused by progressive marginal rates. The sales tax is not regressive because it is not an add-on tax like a state sales tax. It replaces taxes already embedded in the sale price and makes them visible. The only thing it increases is visibility, which helps to protect against increasing rates.

The claim that the poor spend all of their income and therefore will bear more of the burden of a consumption tax is false. They pay these taxes already. They just don't see them and are not aware of them. So this will increase honesty to the poor, in addition to increasing visibility.

Because 100 percent of the constituents of all politicians will pay this tax, we will all have an incentive to keep the rate low.

The Right Way to Do the "Buffett Rule"

If we put party labels and partisan politics aside long enough, can we find common ground between the Tea Party and Occupy Wall Street? If we can, we take a major step forward in advancing true tax reform.

Recently, much has been made of the so-called Buffett rule. The left, whether or not led by Mr. Buffett himself, wants to increase taxes in the name of fairness. There certainly is populist appeal to the sentiment that Warren Buffett should pay more in taxes than his secretary (who, I've heard, is among the 1 percent since her salary is reported to be $200,000 per year . . . but that is a different matter). The opposing view is that our problems today are not the result of too much economic growth, so the goal shouldn't be to reduce economic growth with higher taxes.

9-9-9 is the first reform to actually solve the issue in a way that is good for the economy. In 1977, the Treasury released a report, *Blueprints for Basic Tax Reform*, which outlined many objectives shared by tax reformers to this day. In it, the Treasury call for integration of the individual and corporate income taxes. This essentially means extending partnership treatment to corporations. This is common ground that should be seized.

Under 9-9-9, business net income flows to shareholders and is picked up on their personal returns. The business tax is calculated independent of net income and affects only one line item on the income statement: tax liability.

Not only are all businesses treated the same, but essentially businesses and individuals are treated the same under 9-9-9.

Using some rough approximations for numbers, let's see whether 9-9-9 accomplishes the Buffett rule.

• Warren Buffett's company, Berkshire Hathaway, earned roughly $7 billion through nine months of 2011. For purposes of this example, we will take the liberty of annualizing these earnings at an even $9 billion.

• Buffett holds roughly 25 percent of the outstanding shares, so his share of these earnings would amount to $2,250,000,000. He would report this figure on his tax return.

• Berkshire Hathaway will withhold and remit the 9 percent tax, so this has no cash flow impact on Buffett as the individual taxpayer.

• He earns a salary of $100,000, so his total income—salary plus share of corporate earnings—would be $2,250,100,000.

• Assuming no charitable contributions, he would deduct only the poverty exemption, which, not knowing his household size, we'll say is $15,000. This brings his taxable income down to $2,250,085,000.

• Multiply by the 9 percent tax rate, and Buffett's tax is $202,507,650, all of which has already been paid. Berkshire already remitted the 9 percent on his share of business net income, and withholding took place already on his salary. His after-tax income would be $2,047,577,350.

• His "effective" tax rate is 9 percent. His marginal tax rate is always 9 percent.

• His secretary, meanwhile, would calculate her tax in the same way but with a different outcome. Assume a salary of $200,000, no charitable contributions, no ownership of Berkshire Hathaway stock, and the same poverty exemption of $15,000. Her tax would be 9 percent of $185,000, or $16,650. Her "effective" tax rate would be 8.3 percent. A lower rate than Mr. Buffett, as it should be. Her marginal rate is also 9 percent.

- For fun, let's compare this with a secretary earning closer to the median salary. Assuming $40,000 of income, less the same poverty exemption of $15,000, a tax of 9 percent would be $2,250. This person's effective tax rate would be only 5.6 percent, lower than Buffett's, as it should be.

By integrating the personal income and corporate income taxes in this manner, we have a tax system exactly as it should be. Buffett pays the highest effective tax rate, higher than his well-paid secretary, and a rate 60 percent higher than our example of a more typical secretary.

This allows the system to be progressive but in a productive way, not a destructive way. It also abides by the Buffett rule in a productive rather than a destructive way of growth-killing, job-killing tax increases.

By restoring fairness, by achieving neutrality, by eliminating the most destructive features of our tax code and replacing them with a pro-growth tax code, we can find common ground, even where we might least expect it.

9-9-9 Is the Fair Way to Have a Zero Capital Gains Tax

The capital gains tax is a wall that separates those with ideas from those with capital. It makes no sense to wall off those with ideas. When you harm those with capital, you ultimately harm workers whose livelihood depends on entrepreneurs with ideas.

The capital gains tax is a form of triple taxation. First, before you earn capital gains, after-tax money must be put at risk; this is the first tax. Next, the present value of future after-tax cash flows generated by the capital asset must increase in order to have capital appreciation; this is the second tax. Finally, once the appreciated capital asset is sold for a gain, the current system taxes it a third time.

In Chapter 2, recall that production drives the economy and risk-taking drives growth. The capital gains tax is a tax on both. Finally, the realization of the gain, which necessitates the payment of the tax, is voluntary.

How can you fund the government with a voluntary tax?

This is about as bad as it gets—triple taxation on the engine of growth where the realization of the tax is voluntary. That's stupid.

For anecdotal proof that the correct capital gains tax rate is zero, look at Warren Buffett. He has paid the same capital gains taxes when the rate was 50 percent, 28 percent, 20 percent, and 15 percent. How much has he paid? Zero! I bet he pays the same tax when the rate is zero too.

Ah, but what about fairness? Under 9-9-9, we treat the holders of a capital gain quite similar to the way they are treated under the current system. But instead of damaging the economy in the process, the way the current system does, we improve it. And instead of it being seen as unfair by some, it is done in a way that all of us would consider fair. Here's how.

- Under the current system, the holder of a capital gain can defer the gain as long as he or she wants. As long as the investment remains at risk, the effective capital gain rate is zero.

- Under 9-9-9, as long as the money is held at risk, the capital gain tax rate is also zero.

- Under the current system, once the investment is cashed out, a preferential tax rate of 15 percent is paid. Compare this with the top tax rate on wage income of 35 percent.

- Under 9-9-9, once the investment is cashed out and is no longer held at risk but used for consumption, a 9 percent retail sales tax is paid on that consumption activity—exactly equal to all other taxes, including wages.

Under both systems, capital is not taxed while at risk but taxed when cashed out. However, there are a few critical differences between the current system and 9-9-9, as well as proposals from presidential candidates.

- With a true capital gains tax rate of zero, capital is free to move from less productive investments to more promising ones. This increases capital mobility and efficiency and the growth rate of the economy.

- The current system, and any capital gains tax, locks in a certain amount of capital, reducing its mobility and efficiency and reducing the growth rate of the economy.

- As soon as the investment is cashed out and used for consumption, it will pay a consumption tax. Thus, anyone living off capital gains alone pays the same tax rate as a wage earner.

- Mitt Romney's plan offers a zero capital gains rate for those with the least capital. It therefore offers the least bang for the buck in terms of economic growth. That is because it is based on the class warfare argument rather than on growth considerations.

- Rick Santorum's plan reduces the capital gains rate from 15 percent to 12 percent, but whatever modest improvement that will generate will be swamped by the distortions and misallocation of capital arising from his approach of having big government pick winners and losers. He does this by giving a preferential tax rate only to corporations, not all businesses, and awarding a zero corporate tax rate only to manufacturers. Won't all corporations then try to figure out how to obtain a manufacturing designation? You can bet that most companies would not be able to find a more profitable investment than the amount paid to lobbyists and politicians to obtain the special manufacturing designation. That increases political power exponentially. Further, the 90 percent of businesses that are not corporations will find their best investment opportunity will be converting to a corporation. None of this expands output.

- Even Newt Gingrich's plan, which features the correct capital gains tax rate of zero, would allow Mitt Romney and Warren Buffett to live off their capital gains tax-free. Under 9-9-9, any investment that is cashed out and used for living expenses will pay the same tax as a wage earner.

9-9-9 is the only tax reform plan that has the correct approach to capital gains while at the same time maintaining fairness, because those living off capital gains will pay the same tax rate as wage earners.

Replacing Bad Tax Progressivity with Good Progressivity

The "progressive" marginal tax rate structure accomplishes nothing good. All it does is guarantee mathematically that in times of national expansion revenues to the Treasury grow faster than personal income. Of course, politicians always spend this revenue boom, which locks in a new, permanently higher baseline of spending in the future. Further, it means the tax burden automatically ratchets up on the people. On the flip side, during economic declines, progressive rates cause federal revenues to decline faster than personal income, another mathematical certainty. This means a larger-than-necessary revenue shortfall, which intensifies the cries for higher taxes.

Progressive rates make federal revenues artificially and unnecessarily volatile. If the government does anything important, why create extra volatility in the revenue stream that funds it?

Progressive rates underpin the tendency for ever higher spending and higher taxes. Far from helping ordinary Americans, they serve the sole purpose of greasing the skids for the expansion of government.

If one grants the premise that the tax system should contain some progressivity, there is a better way to go about it. With the poverty exemptions granted under the 9-9-9 plan, the lower one's income, the lower one's effective tax rate. By contrast, the higher one's income, the higher the effective rate. For society as a whole, effective rates will range from zero (actually, a negative number, since the exemption is refundable) to 9 percent based on income. Importantly, the marginal rate remains 9 percent throughout. This is essential, because marginal rates impact incentives much more than effective rates or average rates.

The following table shows the differences in effective rates under 9-9-9 based on income:

Income	$17,000	$30,000	$75,000	$100,000
Less poverty exemption	22,314	22,314	22,314	22,314
Taxable income	-5,314	7,686	52,686	77,686
Tax due at 9 percent	-478	691	4,742	6,992
Effective rate	-2.8%	2.3%	6.3%	7.0%

Figures are rounded. The poverty exemption is refundable, so a negative "tax due" indicates a refund. The poverty exemption is based on a family of four using 2010 figures.

If we must do progressive rates, this is the best way to do them. Making effective rates progressive doesn't harm the economy the way progressive marginal rates do. If we keep marginal rates low, the economy will stay strong, and we will avoid the unnecessary volatility to federal revenues, which will be stable and grow in line with the economy. By taking away the boom-bust cyclicality, we take away the fuel that ratchets up spending and taxes.

Making the United States the Capital of Capital . . . Jobs, Jobs, Jobs

Capital investment drives economic growth and wages. Investment will be exempted under the business tax and the personal tax, so 9-9-9 will be the economic equivalent of a consumption tax. Leveling the playing field for exports will shift investment to the United States. Putting imports on a level playing field with domestic goods will shift demand to domestic goods and shift foreign investment here. Individuals will have no capital gains tax, which releases capital locked up in suboptimal investments. With 9 percent marginal tax rates, individuals will keep 91 cents on their next dollar of income rather than 65 cents. This could increase capital formation by up to 26 cents on each incremental dollar. Not only will there be more capital to invest, but businesses will be able to deduct capital investment. Finally, profits are repatriated without penalty. All of this increased capital formation and the incentives to invest it will ultimately benefit American workers. The capital-to-labor ratio drives productivity, which drives wages. Lastly, labor income will pay the same tax as capital income.

Reducing the government wedge (the tax and regulatory wedge) increases employment and wages. 9-9-9 reduces this wedge where it is most needed, where there is the greatest surplus of labor. The highest unemployment rates are found among the least experienced, the least educated, and the least skilled. These are the people at the lower end of the wage scale. This is where 9-9-9 delivers the most help and does so in an economically productive way.

Making the United States the capital of capital will drive wage growth. Wage growth is a function of productivity growth, and productivity is a function of the amount of capital invested per worker. According to the analysis conducted by Gary Robbins, 9-9-9 will generate growth that is strong enough to create 6 million jobs and push up wages by 10 percent across the board.

FAQs

Let's address some questions that people have raised.

Does the sales tax make it regressive?

As explained earlier, the national sales tax is not an add-on tax but rather a replacement tax. Unlike a state sales tax, which does increase prices, the national sales tax replaces taxes already embedded in the selling price.

For example, a poor mother who buys milk for her hungry baby is already paying these taxes. Are we really doing her a service by continuing the charade that she doesn't pay taxes? Is she better off when she is told she won't pay taxes if she votes for progressives because they will increase costs on businesses?

We do her and all of us a service by converting invisible business taxes into visible sales taxes. Since we all pay this rate, we all have an incentive to keep the rate low. Anything that unites the country behind the same tax eliminates the politicians' ability to divide us.

Since prices are unlikely to change on a net basis, this doesn't shift the burden of taxation. It only increases visibility. If a bottle of water costs $1 today, it will likely cost around 90 cents under 9-9-9; a national sales tax of 9 percent would be applied on top of that. In the end, the out-of-pocket cost will be roughly the same.

This is because marginal production costs will decline. When that happens, prices do not go up. Just ask the technology sector, one known for falling marginal costs. To enforce pricing discipline on businesses, we are enlisting the largest, most powerful, most effective enforcement agency, the one with the best long-term record—the American consumer.

Some may argue that instead of lower costs translating to lower prices, lower marginal cost of production will flow more to higher wages. This doesn't seem like a bad outcome. Whether wages go up more or prices go down more, either way it seems like a good outcome.

You will hear claims that the sales tax is regressive because the poor spend a higher percentage of their income and will therefore bear a larger share of the sales tax. This is flawed in several ways. First, those who say this are quoting the Keynesian concept of "marginal propensity to consume." Does this mean that if you and I earn the same amount of income, and I decide to be thrifty and save, then I have made a sales tax more regressive upon you? Besides, the marginal propensity to consume is based on the idea that consumption drives the economy. It doesn't. We all have to produce before we consume.

Second, why is income the right denominator? This will miss any spending that someone makes out of savings. Don't people save in order to purchase? If Warren Buffett buys another private jet, this time for personal use, he will pay a sales tax. Who is more likely to purchase out of savings? Those who have savings, of course.

Won't 9-9-9 become 15-15-15?

Hardly. The 9 percent rate should be thought of as a ceiling rather than a floor. Strong economic growth is likely to provide revenues to reduce rates further.

The personal tax and the sales tax are both 100 percent visible and paid by 100 percent of the constituents in every congressional district. This takes away the politician's favorite ploy of divide and conquer, which says, "Vote for me, I'll tax the other guy." A politician would have to be willing to raise taxes on every voter.

The notion that the introduction of the sales tax base will somehow make it easier to raise taxes is illogical at best. It rests on the faulty theory that the current counterproductive tax code is somehow constraining the size of government and moving to a pro-growth, productive tax code will somehow end that constraint. That doesn't hold water. This nonsense theory would presume that conservatives want high rates and an inefficient system, because that would make it hard to raise rates further. It is not the system of collecting tax revenue that causes rates to increase. It is progressives who cause rates to increase. There may be no way to stop their impulse of always wanting to raise any tax they can, every chance they get, by as much as they can. So the best thing we can do is make it harder for them to act on their desires.

The more transparent the tax, the more people see what government really costs. The more we know about what it really costs, the less government we will demand. Since we will all pay the same tax and all pay the same rate, we all have the same vested interest in keeping the rate low.

Importantly, 9-9-9 eliminates the damage caused by progressive marginal rates. If the government does anything important (I can think of a few things), why fund it with unnecessarily volatile revenues? Progressive marginal rates guarantee revenues grow faster than personal income during economic expansions and fall faster than personal income during economic declines. This creates an artificial boom-bust cycle of federal revenues that is stupid! The boom-year revenues get spent, locking in a permanently higher baseline spending level, which is unsustainable. In the next economic decline, the revenue shortfall exacerbates the deficit. This unnecessarily gives progressives more chances to call for higher tax rates. 9-9-9 minimizes those opportunities since revenues will be steadier, moving more in line with GDP.

Even if we eliminated the IRS and had a full FairTax, what would stop progressives from desiring to raise the 23 percent FairTax rate? What would stop them from dreaming about special treatment for, say, funny-looking lightbulbs and much higher tax rates on guns and Bibles?

If it were easy to raise taxes, then a Democrat-controlled, lame-duck Congress in 2010 could have sat on its hands and watched tax rates automatically increase on January 1, 2011. As much joy as that might have brought members of Congress to do nothing, the voice of the people was too strong, and they acted to preserve the current rates. With your involvement, we must not ever make it easy to raise taxes.

You have supported the FairTax, so why not pursue that?

I have been one of the biggest supporters of the FairTax for a long time. The FairTax has support at least as strong as the flat tax. Both have considerable merits, but both will lack the necessary support as long as tax reform supporters are divided. As long as we have one side whose plan has a lot of merit pulling against the other side whose plan also has merit, we sentence ourselves to another year of the current code that has no merit. We need to unite FairTaxers and Flat Taxers in order to have real reform.

What is the impact on seniors?

There is no tax on Social Security benefits. Interest and dividends are taxed like wage income, at 9 percent. Double taxation of dividends is eliminated, which is likely to lead to increased dividend payments. There is zero capital gains tax. The death tax is killed. Regarding the sales tax, seniors, like everyone else, already pay that. The only difference is that currently those taxes are embedded in the sales price and 9-9-9 makes the tax visible. The tax burden doesn't increase; only visibility increases. A senior who buys a bottle of water for $1 will likely pay 90 cents and have the 9 percent sales tax apply. On balance, out-of-pocket costs are not expected to increase. Consumers will see to that.

Is it a value-added tax?

The sales tax is sometimes referred to as a value-added tax, or VAT. It is not. It is a retail sales tax modeled after the FairTax. The business tax, if anything, is closer to a VAT. But assuming this is bad is like saying fire is bad. In some cases fire is bad; in other cases it is quite helpful. It is not the label applied to the tax that matters, though. It's how it is constructed and what it does. The VAT has a negative connotation because in most cases it is added on top of a regular income tax code, as in Europe. Of course that would be bad. The business flat tax is a replacement for the corporate income tax, the personal income tax (which many small businesses pay), both the employer and the employee share of payroll taxes, the capital gains tax, and the death tax. By exempting investment, it is equivalent to a consumption tax, which makes it similar to a VAT. Although we achieve it through different means than does a VAT, we exempt exports and tax imports.

Why doesn't Bruce Bartlett like 9-9-9?

First of all, Bruce Bartlett, once part of the Reagan revolution, announced on his Facebook profile that he voted for Obama. (How's that workin' for ya, Mr. B.?)

Aside from that, he must not have read my plan. In his book *The Benefit and the Burden*, Bartlett makes the case for major tax reform: covering the basics, providing the data, identifying the problems, and offering his input on the way forward. However, he totally mischaracterizes my 9-9-9 plan. In fact, nearly every statement is wrong. He claims, on page 181: "Individuals would be taxed on all of their wages without even receiving a personal exemption or standard deduction."

Fact: The 9-9-9 plan has a substantial poverty exemption.

Businesses deduct $15,000 per worker, and individuals exempt the poverty level that corresponds to their family size. Thus the effective tax rate is zero for workers at the poverty level. The effective tax rate increases as income increases, so a worker with income twice the poverty level would have an effective rate of 4.5 percent (half of 9 percent), and as income increases, so does the effective rate until it reaches 9 percent.

This is a better way to make the tax system progressive, because it keeps marginal rates low for all of society. This keeps incentives high.

Bartlett even acknowledges this benefit earlier in his book.

Because the business tax is applied equally to capital and labor, the $15,000 exemption per worker disproportionately benefits lower-income workers. Businesses hire based on the total cost to employ, and taxes represent such a cost. Today, the business must pay 7.625 percent payroll tax on every worker from dollar one to $106,800. For workers with the lowest productivity, this added cost reduces the demand for unskilled labor. 9-9-9 reduces the effective cost to employ lower-skilled workers.

Bartlett claims: "Businesses would be taxed on all of their receipts except for purchases from other firms."

Fact: In addition to that deduction, businesses deduct all capital investment.

In his chapter on the taxation of corporations, Bartlett explains that "the only rational tax treatment of capital [investment] is full expensing, an immediate write-off just like any other routine business expense."

Fact: In the 9-9-9 plan, businesses deduct "net exports."

This means that exports are deducted from the tax base, while imports are added to the tax base (that is, taxed). This eliminates the tax bias that leads to jobs being shipped overseas. On page 200 of his book, Bartlett favors this type of neutrality: "so that goods traveling through different countries bear only the tax imposed in the country of the final sale."

Further, on page 202 he notes that "since the tax would also apply at the border on goods and services that now enter the country tax free, it would shift the tax burden partly onto foreigners. . . . Thus the taxes levied on imports would exceed rebates on exports."

Fact: The final business deduction is the $15,000 labor allowance mentioned earlier.

Bartlett quotes USC law professor Edward Kleinbard, who concluded that "the 9-9-9 plan was equivalent to a 27 percent tax on wage income, which would raise taxes for all except the rich."[15]

In his paper, Kleinbard ignores the poverty exemption detailed above. Of course this will lead one to conclude that my plan will push the distribution of taxes down. We actually push it upward compared with the current tax on labor.

The tables used to calculate the total size of the exemption can be found in the scoring report that was released by the campaign in September 2011 and linked to the campaign website. Kleinbard published his paper in October 2011, well after the release of the poverty exemption amount. All brochures and material describing 9-9-9 indicated under both the business flat tax and the personal flat tax that "additional deductions will be available for empowerment zones."

In November, we rolled out Empowerment Zones (but changed the name to Opportunity Zones to create distance from President Clinton's highly flawed structure that used the same name). The first statement made at the rollout was that by eliminating the capital gains tax and allowing expensing of business capital investment, my plan turned the entire United States into an Opportunity Zone and would make poverty exemptions available across the board.

But by then it was too late: those who only wanted to pounce did not wait for details. Many, such as Kleinbard and those at the Tax Policy Center, produced "research" that excluded the exemptions. Let's give Kleinbard the benefit of the doubt and assume the omission was unintentional. Let's say the campaign's strategy of releasing the total size of the poverty exemption but waiting over a month to detail its specific application was a poor strategy. Even so, if all the materials said "additional deductions" were available, wouldn't one at least inquire? Or wait for the additional information?

In his report, Kleinbard says it will "materially raise the tax burden on many low- and middle-income taxpayers, who today face little or no tax under the income tax, and a 15.3 percent effective payroll tax burden."

Under 9-9-9, income at the poverty level is exempt on both the employee and the employer side. Our effective tax rate at poverty is zero, which is sure lower than 15.3 percent.

At twice the poverty level, the combined burden on the employee and the employer is half of the 9 percent, or 4.5 percent. Counting both sides, which is lower, 9 percent or 15.3 percent?

Kleinbard doesn't note that the burden of 15.3 percent applies only to cash wages and not to dividends or interest. The tax he favors pushes the tax distribution downward. 9-9-9 taxes capital and labor the same under both the business tax and the individual tax. Dividends and interest pay 9 percent just like wages.

Kleinbard claims the sales tax is a wealth tax.

A wealth tax would imply a calculation of net worth times some tax rate. That would be a disaster. It would drive wealth away when we are trying to foster its creation. It would be a huge tax on production. We need to tax consumption. If he calls ours a "wealth tax," then he should at least call it a "consumed-wealth tax," since it only taxes that amount of wealth that is taken from productive endeavor and converted to consumption.

9-9-9 has the advantage of using the sales tax to tax what someone takes out of society, shifting the burden away from taxing what someone puts into society.

Assuming one uses wealth (that is, savings), rather than current income, to purchase something, it pushes the distribution of taxes higher, not lower, as Kleinbard claims elsewhere in his report.

If someone has capital invested and keeps that capital at risk, he or she pays zero tax under 9-9-9. (Note: Bartlett claims that the correct capital gains tax rate is zero.) This isn't too different from the case today, where the holder of a capital gain can choose to defer it indefinitely. 9-9-9 achieves similar treatment, minus the lock-in effect, whereby the tax traps capital and keeps it from funding more productive ventures.

However, as soon as the investment is cashed in and spent, the holder pays a sales tax (as opposed to a capital gains tax). This shifts the burden upward, not downward. This is the most efficient way to shift the burden upward without distorting investment that drives economic growth and distorting behavior through high marginal income tax rates.

9-9-9 achieves the correct capital gains tax, which is zero, while maintaining a system that is fair.

As a show of good faith, I'll point out where Bartlett and I share common ground. After all, we need to unite in order to accomplish real reform, not mischaracterize the plans of other serious reformers, and there is much more common ground when we actually look for it. When I looked, here is what I found:

Bartlett states: "The problem we have today is that there has been a serious divergence between the size of government that people want and what they are willing to pay for."

We agree. The solution is higher visibility of taxes. 9-9-9 makes taxes more visible and transparent. The reason for this divergence is that some think government is free and keep voting for more, not realizing it is costing them jobs and not realizing that they pay business taxes that are embedded in consumer prices. By making some of the invisible business taxes visible, we will all know more about what government costs, and we will therefore demand less.

Bartlett believes tax deductions, or tax expenditures, are for the most part indistinguishable from government spending.

We agree. We get rid of all but charitable deductions.

Bartlett acknowledges we should shift the tax burden more to consumption. He acknowledges there is a long history, dating to at least Alexander Hamilton, of wanting to tax what people take out of society rather than what they put in. He acknowledges that progressive marginal rates create a marriage penalty and attempted fixes just further distort the code.

We get rid of the marriage penalty with one flat marginal rate.

Bartlett acknowledges that a tax system can have flat marginal rates and still have what he calls "de facto progressivity" because of a poverty exemption. This is what 9-9-9 does.

Bartlett acknowledges that the mortgage interest deduction disproportionately benefits the well-to-do, that it is unfair to renters, that it contributes to the overconsumption of housing, and that it reduces labor mobility.

We agree. We achieve neutrality by eliminating the deduction.

Bartlett acknowledges that it is ideal to treat corporations like partnerships, with all profits and losses, whether distributed or not, attributed to owners, which he calls "full integration." 9-9-9 achieves Bartlett's full integration.

Bartlett acknowledges the correct tax on capital gains is zero. And he acknowledges that business capital investment should be fully expensed and not depreciated.

He acknowledges that people with the same lifetime incomes should pay roughly the same tax. 9-9-9 accomplishes this type of fairness. Under the current system, however, a person with steady wages over ten years would pay less in tax than an entrepreneur who earned the same total income but most of it in the last two years.

Bartlett acknowledges that it is not uncommon for the poor to lose a dollar of benefits when they earn a dollar of income, resulting in a tax of 100 percent. This is why we created Opportunity Zones.

Bartlett acknowledges that since half the population does not pay income taxes, it makes it hard to reduce rates. Our solution is to consolidate all taxpayers, income tax and payroll tax payers alike, under the same tax base and same tax rate.

Bartlett acknowledges we gain economic efficiency by reducing tax loopholes.

He acknowledges that a key goal of tax reform should be to provide as much neutrality as possible.

He acknowledges that a sales tax in excess of 10 percent starts to encourage avoidance.

He acknowledges that consumption need not be taxed directly to have the equivalent of a consumption tax. By eliminating investment from the business tax and the personal tax, 9-9-9 acts like a consumption tax.

He acknowledges that taxing imports and exempting exports achieves neutrality.

Integrating 9-9-9 with the Leading Social Security and Health-Care Reforms

Social Security

Social Security benefits are not touched by 9-9-9. Benefits get calculated the same way. All this does is create a more efficient revenue stream to pay for the benefits.

If we later implement a Chilean-style model for having personal ownership of Social Security accounts, taxpayers could elect to direct a portion of their tax payments to personal IRAs in return for waiving some amount of their future Social Security benefits. Since withholding will start at the first dollar, those who elect the personal option will get a deposit from the Treasury to their personal retirement account.

As far as reform, economic growth solves a lot of the problem. Each year growth is under 3.5 percent, the problems of Social Security and Medicare compound, seeming to be insurmountable. With growth above 3.5 percent, those same problems seem quite manageable. Entitlement reform is desirable, but economic growth must come first. Also, Social Security reforms involving means testing must be avoided, or else the program will become nothing more than another income redistribution scheme. The preferred change to the system is to index benefits to inflation rather than wage growth. The underlying problem of the Social Security system is a demographic one where the ratio of workers paying into the system compared with current retirees receiving benefits is the key variable. The current ratio is 4:1, and problems are expected once that level approaches 2:1, as it will in a generation. But why is no one talking about increasing productivity as a solution? Why not have as a goal making those two workers as productive as four workers? I'm not saying we shouldn't reform the system. I'm just saying we need to work on the right problem. We need to start with economic growth and increase worker productivity. 9-9-9 will generate strong growth and improve the capital-to-labor ratio, which raises productivity and wages. Let's do these things first: offer a personal account option and then see how much of a problem still exists. Then we can solve that problem from a position of strength.

Health Care

9-9-9 eliminates the distortion that causes out-of-control health-care costs. Central to health-care reform is the reduction of the government wedge, bringing buyer and seller closer together. Health Savings Accounts (HSA) play a vital role. To the extent that Congress considers an incentive for consumer-driven health care, such as "premium support," my advice would be to avoid creating a tax deduction. The better alternative would be to increase the exemption amount. Presently, every family will get an exemption for the poverty level that relates to family size. This threshold could be increased to cover "poverty plus health care." This keeps deductions clear of the tax code. Since personal tax withholding is expected to start at the first dollar, each household will receive the refundable poverty exemption. This could be directed straight to the taxpayer's HSA. Moreover, if the exemption is increased to a new level, representing poverty plus health care, some or all of the increased refund could be deposited directly into an HSA.

The biggest drivers of health-care costs are diseases such as Alzheimer's, cancer, and diabetes. Nothing must be allowed to get in the way of scientific and medical research to defeat these dreaded diseases.

9-9-9 starts by increasing capital formation. There will be much more capital to invest and more incentives to invest it. Individuals pay zero capital gains, and businesses deduct capital investment. To the extent that capital is a constraining factor for innovation and scientific breakthroughs, 9-9-9 does its part to create the environment most conducive to technological advances.

Chapter 6

Regulatory Reform and the Creation of a Regulatory Budget Office

> *If the public are bound to yield obedience to laws to which they cannot give their approbation, they are slaves to those who make such laws and enforce them.*
>
> —*Samuel Adams*

Do we need to fundamentally transform America? Or fundamentally transform Washington, D.C.?

President Obama has made it clear he wants to fundamentally transform America. The rest of us believe we must fundamentally transform Washington. This is the better way to view the struggle between his 1 percent and the rest of us representing the 99 percent. To transform Washington, we must take power back. Nearly all problems we face can be traced back to the government overstepping the authority of the Constitution and becoming too powerful. There are three places power is taken and abused: the tax code, the regulatory apparatus, and the Federal Reserve. We can't trim around the edges. All three bodies must be fundamentally transformed and power brought back to We the People.

Today, risk-taking is stifled more than ever by the uncertain regulatory environment. Businesses have plenty of risks to deal with, which they do, but not knowing the rules of the game in advance makes ordinary risk-taking impossible. Not being able to keep up with the flood of new rules, regulations, and mandates is the same thing.

This hurts in two ways. First, the overall burden of regulatory compliance increases average costs and drives the government wedge higher. This reduces output, employment, and wages. Second, uncertainty about how regulations will be selectively enforced becomes an unquantifiable marginal cost and affects business decisions at the margin. The solution is a Regulatory Budget Office. This will change the debate over regulation from whether we should regulate—of course we should—to how we should regulate, with full focus on the cost-benefit impact to the private sector, which pays for every penny of every government program at every level of government.

Every bill that is passed by Congress goes to the Congressional Budget Office, where it is "scored"—analyzed to see how much the bill will cost over time. There are plenty of problems with the way the CBO works, but it is the closest thing to real, independent analysis you'll get in Washington.

No such cost-benefit analysis is performed for federal regulations, however. When a new regulation is imposed—either by legislation in Congress or administratively by a federal agency—there is no independent cost-benefit analysis that demonstrates whether the regulation, on balance, does more harm or more good.

That needs to change, and that's what a Regulatory Budget Office would do.

The Economic Impact of Regulation

Estimates of the total cost of regulation on the economy as a whole are quite high. Nicole V. Crain and W. Mark Crain's 2010 study, "The Impact of Regulatory Costs on Small Firms," commissioned by the Small Business Administration, appears to be the best work on the subject.[16] It estimates that the total cost of federal regulations in 2008 was $1.75 trillion, or about 12 percent of GDP. This is more than the burden of personal and corporate income taxes combined! This represents a substantial increase over time, and given the current regulatory environment, it is virtually certain that costs are substantially higher now than in 2008, thanks to passage of Dodd-Frank and Obamacare.

In a new study conducted by the Heritage Foundation, "Red Tape Rising: Obama-Era Regulation at the Three-Year Mark," by James Gattuso and Diane Katz, from the start of the Obama administration to January 2012, "a total of 10,215 rulemaking proceedings were completed. Those included 244 rulemakings classified as 'major,' of which 106 increased burdens on private-sector activity. The estimated cost of these new burdens tops $46 billion."[17] But neither Congress nor the administration keeps tabs on the total number and cost of regulations!

The Heritage Foundation mined the Federal Register and various government databases. Figure 6-1 shows the ever-growing regulatory machine in Washington.

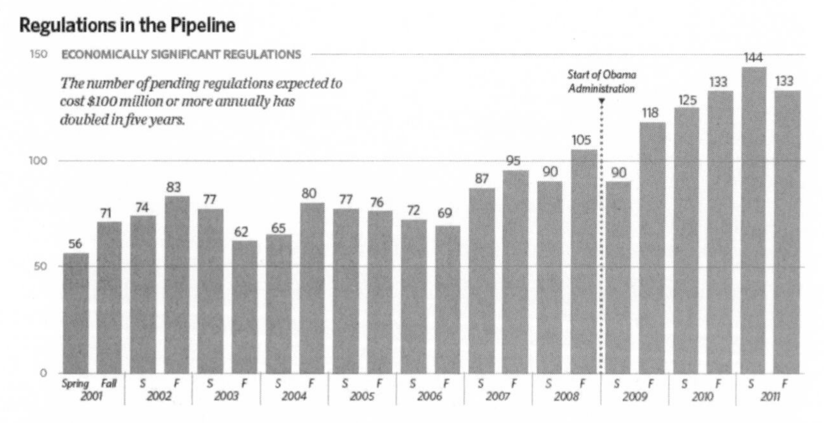

Figure 6-1. More costly regulations in the pipeline. Source: Heritage Fouindation http://www.heritage.org/research/reports/2012/03/red-tape-rising-obama-era-regulation-at-the-three-year-mark

If this isn't scary enough, can you believe that the agencies get to perform their own cost-benefit analysis? They have a natural incentive to minimize or obfuscate the costs of their own regulations. For some, costs are only partially quantified. For others, none are quantified at all. But even quantified costs may often fail to capture the true impacts, as regulators cannot estimate intangibles, whose costs could dwarf the direct compliance burden. One such example is a rule contained in Dodd-Frank. (The truth-in-labeling laws should require this to be renamed Dodd-Frankenstein—but then, why offend Frankenstein?) It required shareholder approval of executive compensation and included the estimated cost of holding a proxy vote. But the far larger cost is the risk of losing executive talent, a cost that is probably unquantifiable but has very real impact.

The fox is guarding the henhouse in Washington. Fortunately, a court struck down the SEC's cost-benefit analysis in this case, stating: "The Commission inconsistently and opportunistically framed the costs and benefits of the rule; failed adequately to quantify the certain costs or to explain why those costs could not be quantified; neglected to support its predictive judgments; contradicted itself; and failed to respond to substantial problems raised by commenters."[18]

The Cross-State Air Pollution Rule, which imposed more stringent emissions limits on power plants in twenty-seven states, estimated the cost at $800 million annually.[19] A number of other sources—some tied to the affected industry, some not—forecast much worse impacts. According to the Brattle Group, the costs of the regulation would total $120 billion by 2015.[20]

Similarly, the EPA pegged the costs of the Boiler MACT at $2.6 billion annually. The Council of Industrial Boiler Owners, on the other hand, estimates that the regulation will entail compliance costs of $14.5 billion.[21]

The National Labor Relations Board (NLRB) likewise minimized the cost of its new rule requiring additional notifications to employees about employment laws. The board contended that the regulation will impose a mere $64.40 per employer, on average, in the first year (for a national total of $386.4 million). An analysis by the law firm of Baker & McKenzie estimated that each private-sector employee will spend at least one hour in meetings related to the regulation, resulting in a productivity loss to the economy of $3.5 billion—almost ten times the NLRB figure.[22]

Who is measuring the cost imposed on the private sector of having to engage in expensive court battles just to rein in unaccountable bureaucrats? Congress must increase scrutiny of regulations—both old and new—including requiring congressional approval of major rules, sunset clauses for each major regulation, and an independent, nonpartisan Regulatory Budget Office.

The Need for Regulatory Reform

Not only is the current system for limiting federal regulation complex; it simply doesn't work. The Administrative Procedure Act,[23] Executive Orders 13422[24] and 13563,[25] the Office of Management and Budget Circular A-4,[26] the Regulatory Flexibility Act of 1980,[27] the Small Business Regulatory Enforcement Fairness Act of 1996,[28] and the Paperwork Reduction Act[29] all have had some positive effect. On the whole, however, agencies have become quite proficient at evading their strictures when they wish to pursue a regulatory agenda. The scope, cost, and intrusiveness of federal regulations continue to grow. That needs to change.

The Regulatory Budget Office

It is clear that the current system of constraints on the costs that federal agencies may impose on society is largely ineffectual. A new system is required. Imposing meaningful restraint on the regulatory actions of federal agencies would achieve large savings and have a dramatic positive impact on economic growth and living standards.

Establishing a Regulatory Budget Office (RBO) would set strict, enforceable constraints on the ability of the federal government to impose regulatory costs on the public. I would like to thank David Burton, general counsel of the National Small Business Association, for helping to formulate this much-needed reform.

This is what would be needed to make an effective Regulatory Budget Office:

1. It would require independent, rigorous, and fact-based estimates of the cost of all existing regulations by agency. This task could be assigned to an existing agency with a record of independence (for example, the Bureau of Economic Analysis at the Commerce Department), although I think a Regulatory Budget Office established expressly for this purpose is best. Either way, it need not be terribly costly. It would probably require about $30 million to $50 million annually, and these costs could be offset to some degree by terminating all the existing positions throughout the government that currently, in theory, conduct cost-benefit analyses.

2. The RBO would have the authority to compel all agencies to provide relevant information.

3. Congress would establish a National Regulatory Budget (NRB), setting a cap on the cost that each agency's regulations could impose.

4. If an agency imposed costs above the NRB cap, it would be required to withdraw regulations until it was below the NRB cap.

5. All new regulations would be required to receive an estimate from the RBO before they could be implemented.

6. Noncompliance by the agency would be subject to judicial review, and the courts would be required to invalidate regulations that caused agencies to exceed their NRB caps.

Chapter 7

Monetary Reform: A Case for Sound Money

> *Don't cheat when measuring length, weight, or quantity. Use honest scales and weights and measures.*
>
> *—Leviticus 19:35*

Overview

A mile is 5,280 feet. Everyone knows that, right? And a pound is 16 ounces. That's easy. An hour is 60 minutes. Of course.

You don't even take a second to wonder about these things. You take them for granted, and you depend on their being true.

But imagine what would happen if the government announced tomorrow that a mile is now 5,900 feet, a pound is now 13 ounces, and an hour is 48 minutes? There would be mass hysteria. But wait. The next day, the government announces that the mile is down 400 feet, the pound is up 1 ounce, and the hour is up 7 minutes. The federal Department of Weights and Measures has decided to engage in "quantitative easing" of distance, weight, and time. If it gets the results it wants, great. If not, the department might change it again tomorrow.

This would be insane, of course. The people would never stand for it.

And yet when it comes to the central linchpin of our entire economy, our money, the government—through the Federal Reserve—does this all the time. It's been doing so ever since we went off the gold standard in 1971. And the result has been disastrous.

In Chapter 2, the third economic guiding principle is "Measurements must be dependable." Without this principle, the others don't matter much. This is what "locks in" prosperity, makes it sustainable, and allows the prosperity to find every corner of society. Without it, economic cycles are more like boom-bust cycles and get short-circuited before they reach the middle class. This gives legitimacy to the frustration and anger that the rich and Wall Street prosper while the middle class struggles, and it is because of the yo-yo dollar.

Sound money and low taxes are like two gears that must both be totally engaged. An engine can't move with one gear operating independently of the other.

Let's imagine that government manipulated time in the manner I described above. Life would be utter chaos. Of course, because of the genius of the private sector, new growth businesses would spring up to help us manage the chaos; I'll call this the Chaos Industry. They would come up with innovative ways to cope and minimize the impact. New devices would be invented to adjust schedules, calendars, and clocks based on the floating measure of time. We would all purchase these new amazing apps for our telephones. We would marvel at American entrepreneurial ingenuity for being so solutions oriented.

Others, like me, would wonder if this was really necessary at all. If something has worked since the beginning of time, no pun intended, then it ain't broke, so don't fix it. The progressives would quickly seize the opportunity to use the floating hour to gradually but continually grab power from the people, claiming somehow that it helps the poor.

Knowing that they had to stand for reelection every two years, Congress members would abdicate their responsibility by fully empowering a newly created board of governors of the mythical "Federal Time Bank" to manage all of our time. This new organization would be totally unaccountable to the voters, but Congress would say that it was "independent" rather than unaccountable since that has a better ring to it. So that the Federal Time Bank could pursue its true but hidden mission of expanding government, these elites who run the Time Bank would (1) be insulated from the unwashed masses and (2) be set up with a "dual mandate" to help people be on time and help people take their time.

Since it is impossible to hit two targets with one arrow, the bank would be free to "independently" pursue its real mandate of feeding big government. Despite insurmountable evidence that this floating hour was causing intolerable destruction to the economy as evidenced by a record-shattering number of missed appointments, missed opportunities, and production gridlock, even after the Chaos Industry's attempts at mitigation, nearly every newsroom, establishment media outlet, and university would sing the praises of the floating hour and opine on the downright restrictive nature of the old barbaric system.

Why, under the old archaic system, people would actually expect you to be on time! The nerve of some people. Those in the Chaos Industry would become fierce defenders of the new system, realizing they owed their existence to this con game. As a share of GDP, the Chaos Industry would get larger and larger. More capital would be diverted to "hedging" the risk of floating time, so fewer ideas would be financed, and growth would slow. Our best and brightest college graduates would go where growth, money, and opportunity awaited, into the Chaos Industry. We would develop a shortage of real engineers and have to look to India. Entrepreneurial ideas that would raise living standards tomorrow would take a backseat to the more immediate priority of anything that could help manage the chaos today. Living standards would stagnate. More and more business would require lengthy contracts that included page after page of legalese designed to address the risk of floating time. And guess what? The intention of the new legal language would be to get the parties to transact as though the hour were still 60 minutes by agreeing to a series of terms and conditions in the event it was not.

GDP numbers would not tell the whole story. They would show growth overall, but these numbers would largely result from the Chaos Industry eating up a greater share of the economy. A look at GDP minus government spending and the Chaos Industry would reveal a declining trend in private-sector production, the engine of the economy. But only "crackpot" economists would look at things that way, because academia would be teaching that government and the Chaos Industry can consume as much GDP as they want without consequence. The affluent would find ways to cope, and then eventually to profit. Morally, philosophically, and politically, they would agree the system was broken and needed to be fixed, but they would not likely break a sweat trying to do so, because it's profitable and, hey, they're just playing by the rules the government sets. Resentment would bubble up from those at the bottom of the economic food chain who were finding fewer opportunities to engage in productive activity while those at the top seemed to have ever more opportunities.

Would the very fabric of society begin unraveling at the seams? Yes, absolutely. And, as you may have guessed by now, I am really talking about the floating dollar. The government's most solemn pledge to its citizens is to maintain the value of the currency. Without that, all else is chaotic. Do you recall the debate in 2011 over the debt ceiling? The mere mention of defaulting on our government debt caused a huge stir, to put it mildly. Well, then, please explain something to me. Since the government has two types of obligations, one interest-bearing and the other non-interest-bearing, why does no one care that we regularly default on our non-interest-bearing notes but all hell breaks loose at the mere mention of default on our interest-bearing notes?

Federal Reserve notes are non-interest-bearing obligations, and Treasury notes are interest-bearing. We routinely debase our currency, and it must stop. If an hour is defined as a fixed quantity of minutes, a mile defined as a fixed quantity of feet, and a pound a fixed quantity of ounces, then a dollar should be defined as a fixed quantity of gold. The Constitution agrees! In article 1, section 8, the Constitution gives Congress—not the Federal Reserve—the authority "to coin money, regulate the value thereof, and of foreign coin, and fix the standard of weights and measures." It doesn't say "manipulate." It says "regulate."

Marxist revolutionary, arch nemesis of free enterprise, and proponent of socialist economic systems Vladimir Lenin is thought to have said: "The surest way to destroy a nation is to debauch its currency."

The economist John Maynard Keynes added this:

> *By a continuing process of inflation, governments can confiscate, secretly and unobserved, an important part of the wealth of their citizens. By this method they not only confiscate, but they confiscate arbitrarily; and, while the process impoverishes many, it actually enriches some. The sight of this arbitrary rearrangement of riches strikes not only at security, but at confidence in the equity of the existing distribution of wealth. Those to whom the system brings windfalls, beyond their deserts and even beyond their expectations or desires, become "profiteers," who are the object of the hatred of the bourgeoisie, whom the inflationism has impoverished, not less than of the proletariat. As the inflation proceeds and the real value of the currency fluctuates wildly from month to month, all permanent relations between debtors and creditors, which form the ultimate foundation of capitalism, become so utterly disordered as to be almost meaningless; and the process of wealth-getting degenerates into a gamble and a lottery. Lenin was certainly right. There is no subtler, no surer means of overturning the existing basis of a society than to debauch the currency. The process engages all the hidden forces of economic law on the side of destruction, and does it in a manner which not one man in a million is able to diagnose.*[30]

One of the major reforms of Cain's Solutions Revolution is to restore sound money—a dollar once again as good as gold.

First, some basics. This can be a complex subject. But thanks to my Uncle Leroy and Aunt Bessie test, I hope to help you grasp the essence.

I have devoted a significant amount of this book to the restoration of sound money, for these reasons:

- It is that important. Arthur Laffer, the economist most

deserving of a Nobel Prize, observes that if regulatory policy is a 1, then tax policy is a 10, and monetary policy is 100.

- The issue is not well understood. But it needs to be. I have made sure to present the material in a basic and straightforward manner.

- I am convinced that sound money is the key to limited government and liberty, more than anything else being talked about, so I am going to talk about it. Without it, we will have neither spending restraint nor middle-class prosperity. And we need both.

Later in the chapter I will present some of the work that my Sound Money Reform Committee originally prepared for my campaign. Rich Lowrie, coauthor of this book, chaired the committee and personally selected my team of economic policy advisers from among the very best monetary policy experts in the country. The cochairs were Chuck Kadlec, Brian Domitrovic, and Paul Hoffmeister. Louis Woodhill, our economic growth specialist, also made important contributions to this policy. They did a superb job and deserve a special acknowledgment here. I hope you appreciate their work as much as I do.

Before diving in, allow me to give you a way to think about monetary policy by painting a couple of pictures that I hope will be worth a thousand words.

There are two thoughts I want you to consider:

1. Goods tend to have a relatively stable relation to each other; it is the currency that causes the price level to change.

2. Since that is the case, we must manage our currency in the best possible way to ensure price stability.

Easy enough, right? Picture a little girl with a lemonade stand. (Assume the government regulators from the FDA will not shut her down. Don't laugh: they closed at least eight last year.) Her handmade sign says "Lemonade, $1." A smooth-talking smoothy, whom I'll call Sharpie, approaches in a fancy car. He orders a cup, and the little girl says, "One dollar, please." Sharpie pulls out a dollar and, knowing his Harvard degree trumps the little girl's third-grade education, slowly rips the dollar in half, as if the girl might not notice, all the while shooting glances over his shoulder to see if any adults are around. Then he hands her one half of the torn dollar bill along with a manufactured smile and says, "Here you go, thank you, little girl."

Astonished but unfazed, the little girl politely says, "I'm sorry, sir, my price is now two dollars!" She thought to herself, "He must think I'm stupid."

Down the street, a little boy has set up a stand selling apples. His price is also $1. Before the "dollar debasement," one apple could be exchanged for one lemonade. After the debasement, one apple will still exchange for one lemonade. The relationship between the two goods didn't change. Only the unit of account, the measuring stick, the dollar, had changed—in this case, a debasement that doubled the supply of money relative to goods, causing the dollar price of all goods to double.

Notice that the price of apples in terms of lemonade did not go up, only the price in terms of dollars. *This is exactly the situation with oil and gas prices today. Those prices are high only in terms of debased paper dollars!*

In a simple neighborhood economy like this, with only two goods, there is one exchange ratio, or price, to keep track of—that of apples to lemonade. But what about our economy, with millions of goods? It is impossible to track all prices this way, and that is why a stable currency is so important.

Given that the above is true—that the prices of goods have a somewhat stable relationship to each other and it is the value of the currency that changes the overall price level—how do we conduct monetary policy to achieve price stability? The reason this is so important is that "price" is one of the most important pieces of information under the sun. The amount of information contained in a single data point is mind-boggling. A Coke costing $1 has information contained within the price about the costs of production, the returns to capital, the returns to labor, taxes, and an amazing assortment of other variables.

You don't have to worry about all that. Just know that prices help allocate everything else in the economy—time, money, resources, and so on. The more "clean" the price signal, the more efficient the allocation of resources, and the more that output and employment can be expanded. If you can think of anything more vital to the optimal functioning of the economy, let me know. If the currency is stable, reliable, and dependable, then changes in relative prices between, say, apples and lemonade send meaningful, actionable signals throughout the economy.

An increase in the price of apples relative to lemonade sends signals that reduce apple consumption and simultaneously increase apple production, resulting in restoration of the original 1:1 relationship. Keeping these signals clean is only accomplished when the dollar is stable, just as an hour is always 60 minutes. A dollar that is unstable causes false signals to ripple through the price system—distorting information, delaying action, canceling out real price signals, misallocating resources, and causing chaos.

Our economy is too large to keep track of the price of an apple in terms of lemonade, because we would also have to keep track of it in terms of gasoline, pencils, wine, and every other good and then track those goods against each other. Without a medium like currency, the number of exchange ratios would quickly become unmanageable.[31]

But with a reliable currency, it doesn't matter how many goods there are, only that the dollar is reliable. When the dollar loses reliability in an economy with millions of prices, now you can appreciate the sheer magnitude of the problem.

So how do we manage the dollar to achieve price stability? The simplest answer is to back the currency with collateral and then let the private economy decide how much liquidity the private economy needs. In the lemonade-and-apples case, if the currency were backed with collateral, Sharpie would be seriously constrained against debasing it. If he did anyway, the little girl could convert the half dollar bill into real collateral having the value of a full dollar, thus removing excess dollars from circulation nearly as soon as they entered the economy.

I start by asking the same basic questions that helped me to be a successful problem solver for my forty years in business: Are we working on the right problem? In this case, we want to know how to determine exactly how much liquidity (that is, how many dollars) the economy needs on a daily basis. To solve a problem, go closest to the source. Why not just ask the economy directly? It's common sense. It's either that, or we continue to empower elites like Sharpie to decide. You may wonder how we actually "ask" the economy? The overall economy is nothing more than the household economy multiplied by the number of households, or the individual economy multiplied by the number of individuals, or the company economy multiplied by the number of companies. If these entities could register their votes in real time each day, we would have the most precise and timely measurement of the overall economy's demand for liquidity. It is the sum total of your need, plus my need, and so on.

My 21st Century Gold Standard does exactly that. It is a real-time, decentralized, bottom-up, fully accountable monetary system capable of being immediately responsive to the individual needs of the economy's participants. This compares with the top-down, time-delayed, highly centralized, bureaucratic, unaccountable monetary system that is totally incapable of being responsive to individual needs.

In operation, under the modern approach I favor, the actions of the few benefit the many, whereas under the elitist system we have now, the actions of the few benefit only that few.

Consider: Today, if the Fed prints too much money, those sophisticated enough to first identify, then "hedge" this risk are the only ones making money; the rest of us are harmed by a hidden and silent tax called inflation (or deflation). I also call it a sneak-a-tax.

Ever wonder why Wall Street donates big to both Republicans and Democrats? Why Washington (and the media, the universities, Wall Street, and so on) would claw and scratch to oppose restoring sound money? The current system is way too profitable for them. Under the more liberty-oriented approach of a modern gold standard, if the Fed prints more dollars than the economy needs, ordinary citizens will convert those surplus dollars into the more valuable collateral, which removes dollars from circulation. In this case, the actions of those few individuals benefited the rest of us.

Which system seems more compatible with liberty? I trust the people. My solutions empower the people, and it is time to vest the stewardship over the stability of the dollar in the people. Given a choice, the people prefer a stable dollar, and so does the economy. The profits of the Chaos Industry will decline, but prosperity for the rest of us will expand.

Figure 7-1 shows the price of gold and its purchasing power against consumer goods and commodity goods.

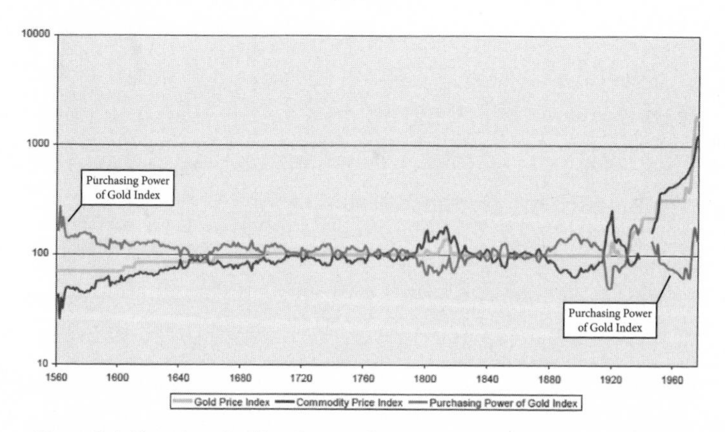

Figure 7-1. The price of gold and its purchasing power against consumer goods and commodity goods; 1930 = 100. (R. W. Jastram, The Golden Constant; The English and American Experience 1560–1976, New York: John Wiley and Sons, 1977.)

This is comparable to the apple maintaining its purchasing power against lemonade in our neighborhood economy. In gold's case, the track record covers 1560–1976. By ending the period where it began, it held its purchasing power for an incredibly long period: over four hundred years. If we want the dollar to hold its purchasing power, it makes sense to back it with gold. If it wasn't broken for more than four hundred years, why did the politicians break it?

Figure 7-2 provides a closer look at the value of the dollar when it was backed by gold compared with when it floated as a paper currency managed by government elites. Uncle Leroy and Aunt Bessie do not need to know a thing about monetary policy to pinpoint when the United States had sound money and when it did not. See if you can tell too.

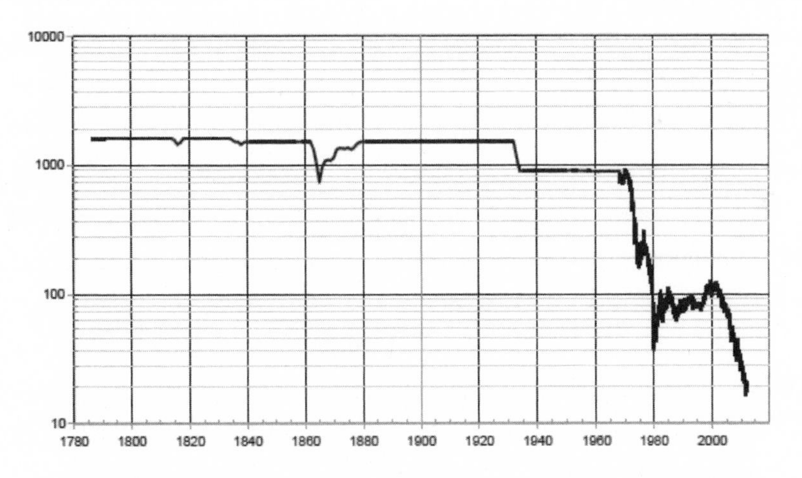

Figure 7-2. U.S. dollar valued in milligrams of gold: January 1787 to February 2012. Source: Priced in Gold http://pricedingold.com/

Our country was established under sound money. In the classic era, which runs until 1913, ordinary citizens could convert paper for collateral, and the system functioned well. It coincided with the longest period of economic growth and prosperity the world has ever seen. Figure 7-3 provides a close-up of economic growth in the pre-1913 sound money era.

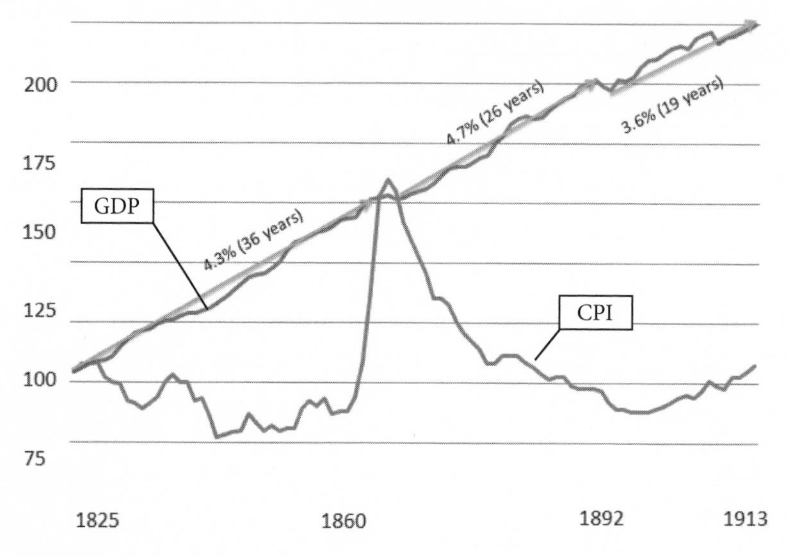

Figure 7-3. U.S. GDP and price level, 1825–1913. Source: Brian Domitrovic

The economy grew at 4.25 percent for more than eighty years, and prices ended that period in the same place where they began. That's called prosperity!

In 1913, the always benevolent progressives gave us the Federal Reserve, which took over management of the gold standard. They promptly messed it up in 1914, which led directly to the devaluation in 1933. During the period that followed, the Bretton Woods era, there was an international gold standard. That worked well, despite some flaws, until President Johnson began printing dollars to expand big government. The surplus dollars created pressure on the system, and instead of reining in spending and removing surplus dollars, President Nixon permanently suspended gold convertibility beginning in 1971. Figure 7-4 gives us a closer look at the post-1913 era.

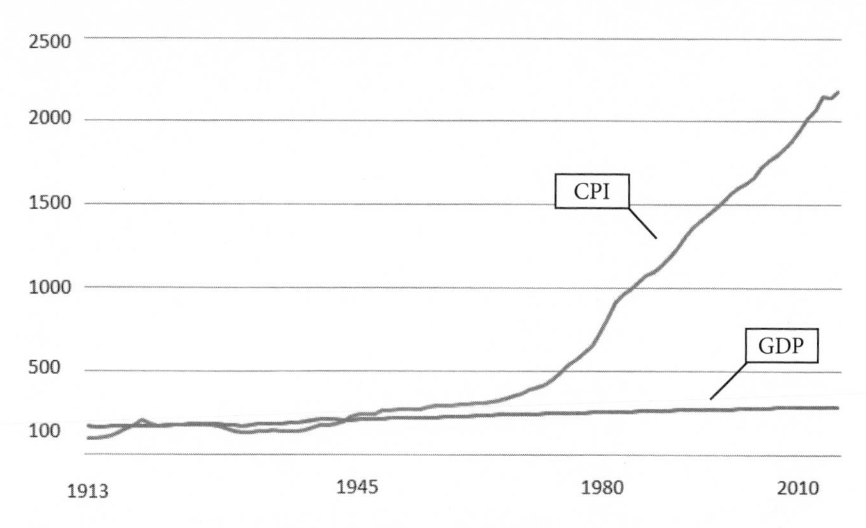

Figure 7-4. U.S. GDP and price level, 1913–2010. Source: Brian Domitrovic

Growth is slower and prices have increased twentyfold. But don't worry, nobody got hurt because the progressives were out to help the poor. Slow growth and ever-increasing prices both crush the poor and create more of them.

The governmental and academic elites and the progressives will fight my sound money reform tooth and nail because the Fed is the handmaiden of big government. Economic historian and Cain campaign economic adviser Brian Domitrovic makes a compelling case for this viewpoint in his paper "The Secret Term in the Fed's Triple Mandate: A Critical History."[32]

By now, most are aware of the Fed's dual mandate: concern for price stability and for full employment. This, Domitrovic points out, owes its existence to the Federal Reserve Act of 1913, the Employment Act of 1946, and the Humphrey-Hawkins statute of 1978. Since the Fed has only one lever to pull, monetary policy, it is impossible for it to hit two targets with one arrow. This frees it to hit the third target, which Domitrovic refers to as the secret mandate, which is to grease the skids of big government with loose money. This amounts to a secret default.

The Secret Default

Remember all the fuss around the debt ceiling? Forget that those politicians really didn't cut anything. What is amazing to me is how absolutely unified the country was behind not defaulting on our interest-bearing debt, while we watch our non-interest-bearing debt get debased in front of our very eyes. Currency is a Federal Reserve note, just like a Treasury note, except it doesn't pay interest. Monetary policy in its most basic form is simply adjusting the ratio of interest-bearing notes outstanding to non-interest-bearing notes outstanding to suit the demands of the economy.

We should never default on any government note, interest-bearing or non-interest-bearing. Period. In the real world, what do you do with deadbeats who can't keep their promises and make good on their notes? That's right, you make them post collateral. That is all that is required of a modern gold standard.

Figure 7-5 shows the secret default that has occurred since the Democrats won control of Congress in 2006.

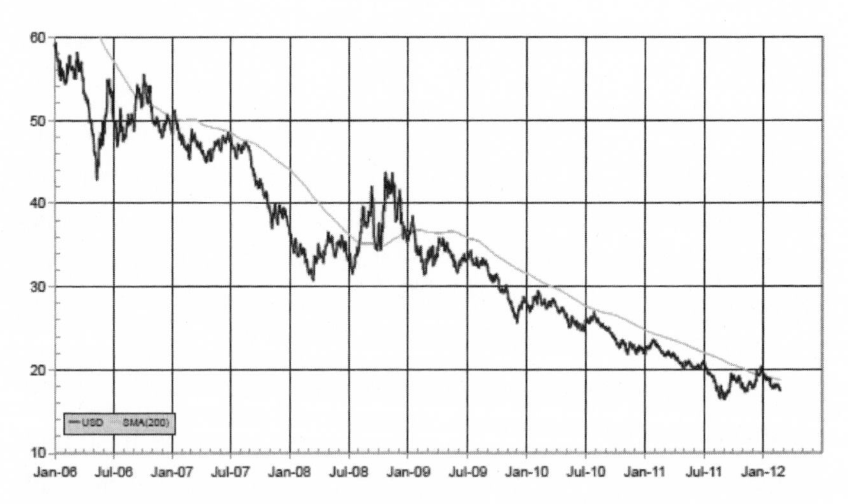

Figure 7-5. U.S. dollar in milligrams of gold, January 2006 to February 24, 2012. Source: Priced in Gold http://pricedingold.com/

It may not get me invited to the next Federal Reserve alumni reunion party, but it is the truth. If the dollar is supposed to hold its value the way an hour is supposed to always equal 60 minutes, then it doesn't take a monetary policy expert to see this sucker is heading in the wrong direction. A weak dollar is not a sign of a strong America.

But doesn't the Fed say it is the job of the Treasury to manage the dollar? And doesn't the Treasury say it is the job of the Fed to manage the money supply? Yes. They do that for a reason: to confuse you! Allow me to clear things up. The Fed's job should be to maintain the value of the dollar relative to domestic goods. The job of the Treasury is to maintain the value of the dollar against foreign currencies.

"But, Mr. Cain," you say, "doesn't that mean fixed exchange rates?"

May I explode another progressive myth? Fixed exchange rates are good. They impose discipline on politicians. We have right under our very noses the best system of fixed exchange rates ever known. It is so good, in fact, you might not even notice it. If it is so good that I have to point it out to you, that means it is doing its job of promoting economic efficiency, and economic efficiency means expanded output and employment.

We have twelve Federal Reserve districts. Each has its own currency. Find a one-dollar bill. The letter code on the left-hand side of the face of the bill shows which Federal Reserve district issued that note. We have a system of fixed exchange rates where all Federal Reserve notes are convertible on a one-to-one basis into all other Federal Reserve notes, no matter which Federal Reserve bank they're from: Cleveland Fed, Kansas City Fed, or any other. In fact, this system is so rigid, so ironclad, that no one even notices it or thinks of it as a system of fixed exchange. The result? The flow of goods and services is very efficient in the common currency area, so much so that we don't even track trade deficits in this area. What would be the point of tracking the trade imbalance between, say, Texas and Ohio?

The problem in Europe is not fixed exchange rates. It is that some countries—for instance, Greece—have used the benefit of fixed exchange rates to overspend. Fixed exchange rates brought a convergence of interest rates and inflation rates. Instead of using the cost savings of lower inflation and interest rates to reduce debt, the worst offenders increased spending. Let's say you had a credit card charging you 8 percent and I had one charging me 18 percent. Then we both formed a "common card" (like the euro), which resulted in cost savings for me. If I used my cost savings to find more ways to spend, you would start calling me Greece. Does anyone think the way for California to solve its debt problems is for the San Francisco Federal Reserve to devalue its notes and pay its bondholders in debased currency?

Once the dollar is backed with gold, a fixed exchange rate should be established with the euro and the yen. Take a look at what is happening to paper currencies today without the gold anchor (Fig. 7-6).

Figure 7-6. Comparison of the price of the U.S. dollar, the Canadian dollar, the euro, and the Swiss franc in gold grams, January 2, 2006 to February 10, 2012. Source: Priced in Gold http://pricedingold.com/

What does this mean to the typical person on Main Street? Let's look at oil prices. Can you tell from Figure 7-7 when paper dollars were backed by collateral and when they were backed only by the politicians' promises? Like Uncle Leroy, even if you don't think you know anything about monetary policy, I bet you can identify exactly when the collateral was removed and replaced by empty promises.

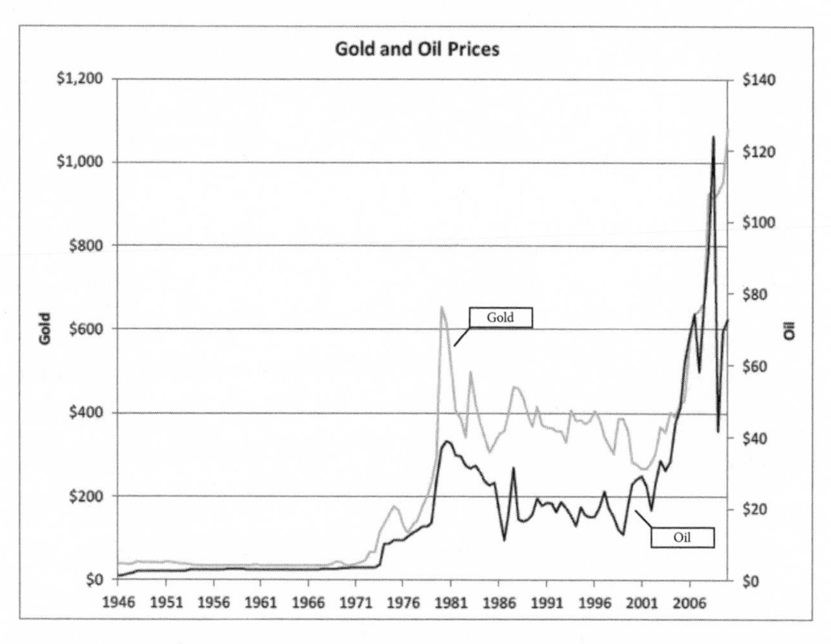

Figure 7-7. Comparison of gold and oil prices, 1946 to the present. Source: Paul Hoffmeister

Even though this is a dated chart, Figure 7-7 is still one of my favorites. Today, gold has moved much higher than the $1,000 level shown here to about $1,700, and oil has moved from the $70 level here to well over $100. But nobody gets hurt when the progressives help us, right? Note that OPEC didn't exist in the sound money period. It was only formed when the empty paper dollar era started. The Arab oil embargo was in response to the weak dollar. The more we diluted our dollars, the more dollars OPEC demanded for a barrel of oil. Just like the lemonade stand example.

Figure 7-8 shows what oil prices would look like if we still had sound money. Of course prices would be volatile but around a flat trend, meaning the dollar would have maintained its purchasing power against oil over all these years.

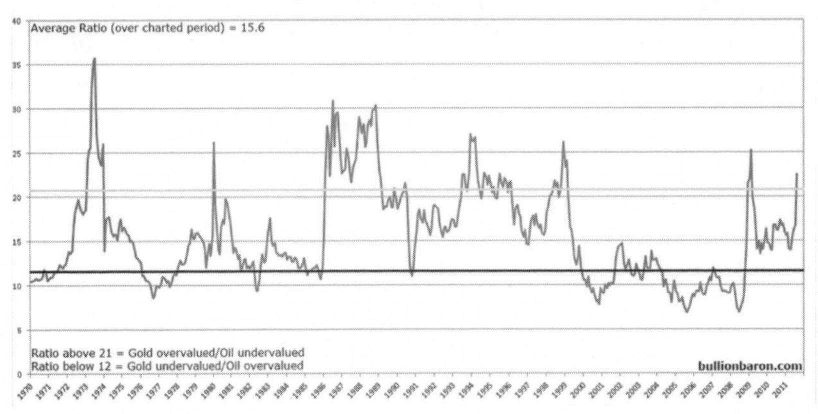

Figure 7-8. Ratio of gold to oil over a 40-year period. ("Gold/Oil Ratio: Where Is It Heading? BullionBaron, http://www.bullionbaron.com/2011/08/goldoil-ratio-where-is-it-heading.html.)

What about gas prices? They are not high! Paper dollars are too weak.

Sound money is synonymous with hard currency. What does that mean? Coins were made out of metals that gave them real value. Pennies contained copper, nickels contained, well, nickel, and dimes and quarters contained silver. Dollars could be converted into various combinations of these coins—or into gold.

Not so anymore. If we hadn't debased our currency, would gas prices be expensive? If dimes still contained 90 percent silver, two dimes, because of their silver content, would be worth roughly $4, about what a gallon of gasoline is selling for in most places (Fig. 7-9).

Figure 7-9. Price of gasoline in pre-1964 coin. (Gary Gibson, "Why Gas Prices Are Actually Falling," http://whiskeyandgunpowder.com/why-gas-prices-are-actually-falling/#hl-gasoline%2020%20gallon.)

Historically, for as long as dimes contained 90 percent silver, a gallon of gas sold for roughly two dimes. That was true in 1918, in 1928, and in 1948. Today, a gallon of gas is still worth two silver dimes. If pennies were still made of copper, a gallon of gas would cost around $1.25. That is because 125 copper pennies would have a value of $4 in terms of copper, enough to buy a gallon of gas.

Figure 7-10 shows the price of a gallon of gasoline if we had sound money.

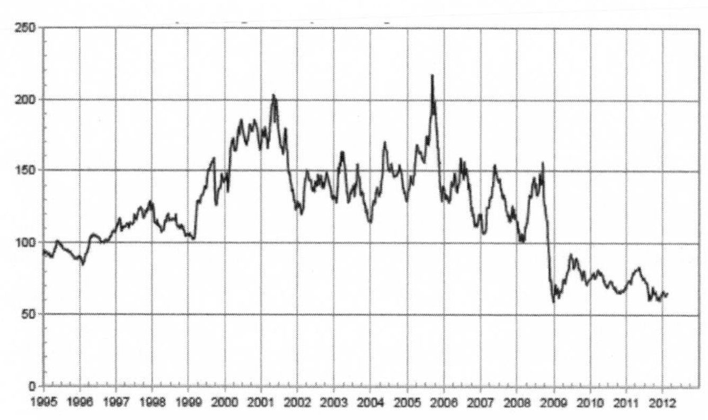

Figure 7-10. U.S. retail gasoline prices in mg of gold per gallon: January 1995 to February 2012. Source: Priced in Gold http://pricedingold.com/

Looked at another way, Figure 7-11 shows gas prices in terms of other consumer goods (gray line), just as we looked at an apple in terms of lemonade, and in terms of paper dollars (black line).

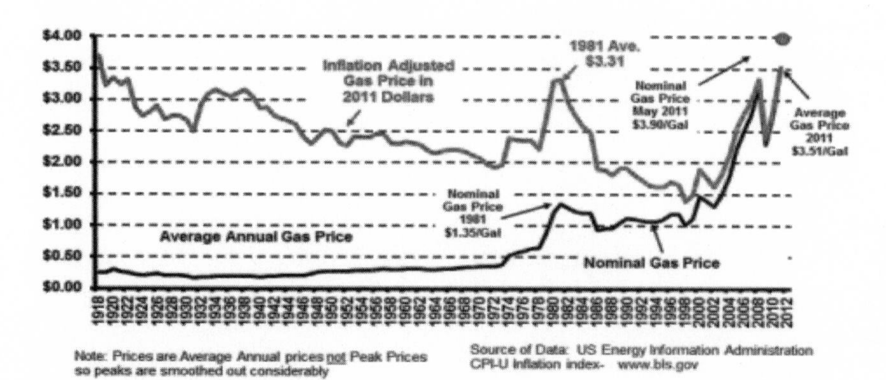

Figure 7-11. Gasoline prices 1918–present, adjusted for inflation. (Timothy McMahon, prepared for InflationData.com, updated June 16, 2011.)

Gas prices are about the same against other goods, just like the apple and lemonade example, but they are ten times higher in paper dollar terms. So, did gas prices go up, or did the paper dollar get debased by Sharpie?

The oil industry should be the biggest advocate of sound money. It would gladly trade an ever-rising and more volatile price for one that was stable. A stable unit of measure, a sound dollar, would allow the industry to invest more capital because the risk of a wide swing in the commodity price wiping out its investment would be virtually eliminated.

Food prices are rising across most categories, with various meat and dairy products registering double-digit gains. The politicians' answer to this is to exclude food and energy prices from the inflation figures. Figure 7-12 shows what food prices would look like if we had sound money.

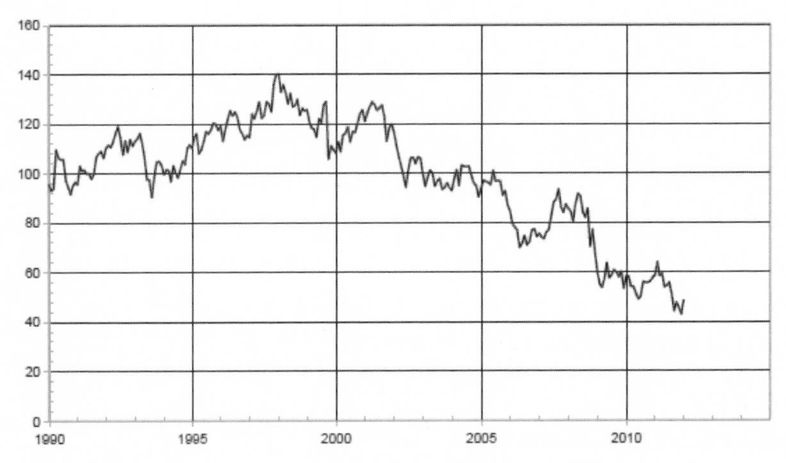

Figure 7-12. FAO food price index in gold: 1990–2012. Source: Priced in Gold http://pricedingold.com/

If you put it all together, here is what it means for the American family. The next picture is worth at least a thousand words. If we measure median wages not in empty paper dollars but in sound money, this is what it looks like (Fig. 7-13).

Figure 7-13. Production worker's hourly wages in gold. (BLS Series CES0500000008, monthly from January 1965 to January 2012.) Source: Priced in Gold http://pricedingold.com/

The more we debase our currency, the more middle-class wages stagnate. But nobody gets hurt when the progressives help us, right? The only period in which the middle class felt prosperous was from 1980 to 2000—a period characterized by tax cuts and a relatively stable, reliable dollar. The gears were engaged and the engine was humming. In 1971, when the real collateral was replaced by political promises, real hourly wages began the sharpest decline, necessitating dual-income households just to keep pace.

Lately, things are as bad as they've been in over a generation, reaching a level not seen since Jimmy Carter. No wonder, we are following the Carter playbook of Weaken America First.

The bottom line can be summed up in a measurement of household net worth. Figure 7-14 explains the anger among both the Tea Party and Occupy Wall Street.

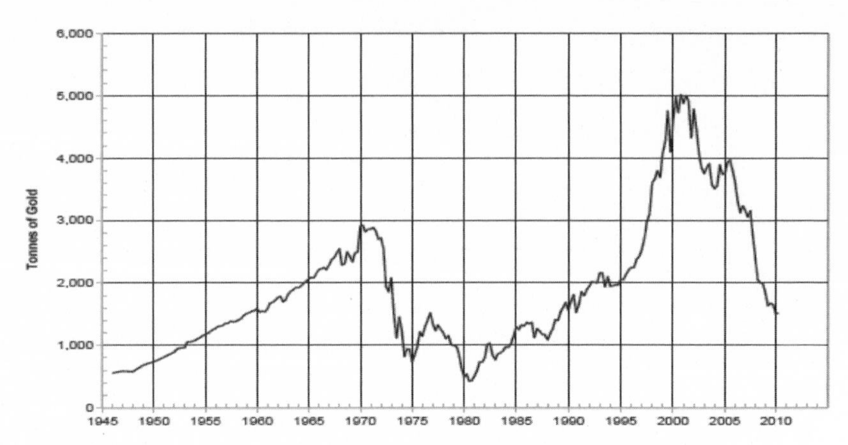

Figure 7-14. Total U.S. household net worth in gold. (Federal Reserve Table Z1/Z1/FL152090006.Q.) Source: Priced in Gold http://pricedingold.com/

A return to sound money needs to be the rallying cry that unites these two groups. Of course, by adjusting the length of the measuring stick, politicians can attempt to deceive. But Figure 7-14 is the real measure of household net worth, in sound money terms.

Notice that the chart begins in 1945, roughly the starting point of the Bretton Woods "sound money" era. Because of sound money, the benefits of economic growth allowed for a steady increase in U.S. net worth. This was crushed by the Johnson, Nixon, Ford, and Carter administrations, the Murderers' Row of economic policy. Since 2000, things have been going in the wrong direction because for some unexplained reason the progressives in both parties favor a weak dollar. Wait! We know the reason. To expand big government.

Even former president Bill Clinton has noticed that wage differentials have widened since we left the gold standard.[33] Want to identify the real culprit behind the middle-class squeeze? It is dollar debasement. The wealthy have the means to hedge against its devastating impact. Of course, if you had the means to protect against it, why not go a step further and look to profit from it? The rich are rich because they ain't stupid. We need to get off this treadmill of progressive policies: first hurting the middle class, then promising to go after the rich, then pursuing policies that weaken the dollar, which hurts the middle class, and the cycle goes on and on. That is stupid.

Household net worth had two sustained periods of prosperity. The first is when we linked the dollar to gold after World War II—the Bretton Woods era. With a dollar as good as gold, all prosperity fell to the bottom line. Notice how it ended as soon as Nixon closed the gold window. Reagan restored sound money policies, although he fell short of his goal to return to gold convertibility. It is widely understood that the Federal Reserve during Reagan's administration operated under a "price rule," meaning it conducted policy in a rules-based fashion according to real-time market-based indicators such as gold, commodity prices, and the dollar's foreign exchange value. Clinton continued this run of prosperity with tax cuts that strengthened the dollar against gold. Since then, we have had the combination of falling asset prices and a falling dollar.

For the real shocker, a sound dollar would buy as much college tuition as it did in 1900 (Fig. 7-15). Can the paper dollar, backed only by the empty promises of politicians, say that?

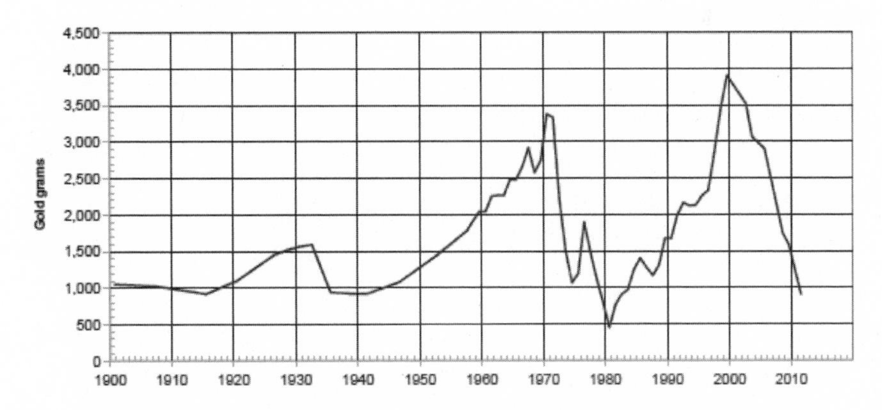

Figure 7-15. Yale college tuition, room and board, in gold grams. (Yale Book of Numbers, news reports: 1900–2011.) Source: Priced in Gold http://pricedingold.com/

Sound Money and Prosperity

Real Growth

The gold standard is the time-tested way to make the dollar always worth a dollar. The benefits of a gold standard are crystal clear: it simply works better than the paper dollar standard we have been on for the past forty-plus years.

Throughout American history, when the American economy has grown at its highest rates, and the American people have achieved their greatest increases in living standards, the United States has been on a gold standard.

The Coinage Act of 1873 effectively put the United States on the gold standard. The Resumption Act of 1875 returned the dollar to its pre–Civil War parity of $20.67 an ounce on January 1, 1879. We pick 1873 as the starting point, because the Coinage Act of 1873 triggered a deflation and a panic. Nevertheless, real GDP grew an average of 4.3 percent a year for the next twenty years. The economy also grew at an above-average 3.7 percent a year from 1873 to 1913.

Here are the data for GDP growth from 1873 to 1913.

Gross Domestic Product, 1873–1913

	1873–1913	Year
High	9.7%	1890
Low	-10.8%	1908
Average	3.7%	

If the U.S. economy had grown an average of 3.7 percent a year since 1913, it would be 60 percent larger today.

Under the post–World War II gold standard, the U.S. economy grew nearly 4 percent a year and the middle class prospered. Since Nixon broke the final link with gold in 1971, GDP has been less than 3 percent—25 percent slower—and real incomes have stagnated.

Gross Domestic Product, 1947–1967 and 1971–2010

	1947–1967	Year	1971–2010	Year
High	8.7%	1950	7.2 %	1984
Low	-0.9%	1958	-3.5 %	2009
Average	4.1%		2.8 %	

If the United States had continued to grow at its gold standard rate, the economy today would be 50 percent larger—average incomes would be about 50 percent higher, and we wouldn't be struggling with a budget deficit.

Real Median Family Income

Real median family income would be much higher, as this table shows.

Real Median Family Income, 1948–1967 and 1971–2010

	1948–1967	Year	1971–2010	Year
High	8.3%	1953	4.9%	1973
Low	-2.6%	1949	-3.4%	2008
Average	2.7%		0.5%	

In 2010, GDP in 2005 dollars was $13,088 billion. If GDP had grown at 4.068 percent per year starting in 1971, it would be $21,022 billion (1970 RGDP = $4,266). Percent increase: 21,022/13,088-1 = 61 percent.

Note, this calculation is sensitive to the starting year. If the starting year is 1947, the growth rate is 3.8 percent, and the GDP is 46 percent larger.

Low Unemployment

During the 1950s and 1960s, when the United States was last on a gold standard, unemployment averaged less than 5 percent, and on an annual basis it never exceeded 7 percent. Since 1971, when the United States stopped guaranteeing the dollar in terms of gold, the unemployment rate has averaged more than 6 percent. As of this writing, it has been near or above 9 percent for nearly three years.

Civilian Unemployment Rate

	1948–1967	Year	1971–2010	Year
High	6.7%	1961	9.7%	1982
Low	3.0%	1952	4.0%	2000
Average	4.8%		6.3%	

Price Stability

What now sounds like an economic miracle was produced with 2 percent inflation. That means when Uncle Leroy and Aunt Bessie got a pay raise, their standard of living went up instead of just running on a treadmill trying to keep up with rising prices and the falling dollar. Since we broke the dollar-gold link, consumer price inflation has averaged 4.4 percent, and the overall price level has gone up more than fivefold! That means a dollar today is worth less than two dimes of a 1971 dollar.

Consumer Price Inflation

	1948–1967	Year	1971–2010	Year
High	8.1%	1948	13.5%	1980
Low	-1.2%	1949	-0.4%	2009
Average	2.0%		4.4%	

In 1970, the consumer price index was 38.8. In 2010, it was 218.506. Price increase: 218.506/38.8 = 5.6.

Stable Interest Rates

Under the gold standard, interest rates are reliably low and stable, providing a fair return to savers and ample credit for businesses to expand, families to get mortgages, and economic growth to be fueled.

AAA Corporate Bond Yields

	1948–1967	Year	1971–2010	Year
High	5.5%	1967	14.2%	1981
Low	2.6%	1950	4.9%	2010
Average	3.8%		8.2%	

Financial Stability

During the entire post–World War II gold standard era, with all of the radical developments in the world economy, there were no financial crises in the United States until President Johnson began to break the promise that a dollar was worth one-thirty-fifth of an ounce of gold. Since abandoning gold for a paper dollar, the American people have suffered through a dozen financial crises, culminating in the financial crisis of 2008 and 2009 and now the European sovereign debt crisis.

1. 1973 oil shock

2. 1979 dollar crisis, second oil shock

3. 1982 Latin American debt crisis

4. 1984 Continental Illinois Bank collapse (largest in U.S. history prior to 2008 financial crisis)

5. 1987 stock market crash

6. 1989–1991 savings and loan crisis and bailout

7. 1990 Japanese bubble collapse and banking crisis

8. 1994 Mexican peso crisis

9. 1998 Asian currency crisis

10. 2001 dot-com crash

11. 2007–2009 housing collapse and international financial crisis

12. 2010–2011 European sovereign debt crisis

Making the dollar as good as gold will bring order and stability to our monetary system and contribute to the prosperity and liberty of the American people. When you provide stability to the financial infrastructure of our economy, the private sector and business do what they do best: invest in the future, create new jobs, produce economic growth, and lift the living standards of American workers.

The Gold Standard Will Lead to Growth

Here are four ways the new gold standard will lead to economic growth:

1. The Fed is required to provide all the money the economy needs to fuel real growth without inflation.

2. When you save, you can do so knowing that the dollar you save will be worth a dollar when it is needed in the future to pay for your child's education or for your own retirement.

3. Those who invest and create jobs can do so without the fear that monetary instability and financial crises will destroy the value of their investments.

4. Investments in real, job-creating businesses will replace sterile investments in hedges against dollar depreciation including gold, foreign currencies, and the like.

When you add it up, a gold standard means prosperity. Prosperity is more than just more money. Prosperity increases our liberty by increasing our capacity to take care of ourselves, our families, and our communities.

America became the strongest, most prosperous nation in the world under a gold standard. Making the dollar worth a dollar by making the dollar as good as gold is a key element to restoring our economic strength and prosperity in the twenty-first century.

Because we ain't stupid, the people understand this. In fact, support for the gold standard is nearly as strong as it is for 9-9-9. In his Forbes column, Ralph Benko breaks down an October 2011 Rasmussen poll showing 44 percent of likely voters favor returning to the gold standard, with 28 percent opposed.[34] When the public knows that it would "dramatically reduce the powers of bankers and the political class to steer the economy," support goes up to 57 percent while opposition drops to 19 percent. Because the gold standard would reduce the power of central bankers and politicians, support for it is widespread among nearly every demographic group. Of particular interest, a majority of African Americans, most with enthusiasm, support the gold standard, as does a majority of union members (including Mr. Benko, a member of the AFL-CIO).

Chapter 8

A 21st Century Gold Standard[35]

How Do We Restore Sound Money?

Below I present the principles of monetary reform and a specific plan to achieve it. Thanks again to Chuck Kadlec, Brian Domitrovic, Paul Hoffmeister, and Louis Woodhill for helping me develop this solution.

My vision for monetary policy and economic growth includes the following:

- Economic growth and prosperity require sound money.

- The greatest runs of economic growth in American history have been periods of stable prices, a strong dollar, and a dollar tied to gold.

- A democratic society must have a monetary system and monetary institutions that win the respect of the public.

There are four monetary guiding principles.

First, the dollar must be strong and stable with respect to the price level, major foreign currencies, and commodities, including gold and oil.

- The claim that there is a trade-off between sound money and unemployment is wrong. When the dollar is as good as gold, we will have low unemployment and inflation.

- Exports and foreign investment boom under sound money. Second, the views of the public must be respected in the conduct of monetary policy.

- The Federal Reserve must take into account market "votes" on the soundness of the dollar, above all the price of gold.

- The International Monetary Fund must be reduced to its proper role of ministering only to midsized countries wanting to cooperate with its member countries regarding the 21st Century Gold Standard.

Third, we must end money creation for illegitimate purposes.

- Today the Fed prints money to fund government debt.

- It prints money to fill balance sheets of mismanaged banks and corporations.

- It prints so much money for these illegitimate purposes that much of it migrates to gold and other hedges against inflation.

- Money creation must provide only as much money as the real economy needs to grow without monetary inflation or deflation.

And fourth, money must be a good and useful agent for all of society.

- Ordinary savers must be able to expect their savings to hold value.

- Interest at banks should reflect the actual cost of forgoing current consumption.

- The financial sector of the economy must and will shrink under the 21st Century Gold Standard in proportion to its real importance as the production of goods and services grows in turn.

Monetary Reform Plan

Monetary reform has two distinct components:

- The first is the transition to a new gold standard, including the discovery of the new fixed rate of exchange between the dollar and gold.

- The second is the design and specification of a new set of operating rules the Fed will use to sustain the new gold standard in a manner that guarantees the value of the dollar in terms of gold, without manipulating interest rates, and that requires the Fed to provide all the money the economy needs to fuel rapid economic growth without inflation.

The ideal end point is an international monetary system with the dollar and other key currencies, including the euro, the Chinese yuan, the British pound, and the Japanese yen, convertible into gold. That includes the circulation of U.S. minted gold coins of a defined weight and purity with a specified dollar value circulating as legal tender in the United States.

Other major countries interested in sound money, including Russia, Brazil, India, and Canada, would also be invited to join. The United

States must be willing to lead, however, by making clear its intention to make the dollar as good as gold with the dollar defined as a fixed weight of gold.

The Transition to a New Gold Standard

Six principles will guide the transition to a new gold standard.

1. Overall prices should remain near today's levels, including no forced reduction in wages.

2. The process for establishing the new link between the dollar and gold must be transparent, making use of markets to establish the value of the dollar in terms of gold.

3. The transition must be gradual, but the path must be clear. This will permit as smooth an adjustment process as possible.

4. The Fed will be given new operating procedures to ensure that under the new gold standard, it will guarantee the value of the dollar and will not restrict the number of dollars available for the economy to grow.

5. Individuals must have the right to exchange currency and deposits at the Fed for gold at a fixed price and, conversely, exchange gold coins and bullion for dollars at the same price.

6. The United States should lead the effort to create a new 21st Century International Gold Standard.

The following steps could be used to implement a gradual transition with a clear path toward "making a dollar worth a dollar."

Set a Date

Announce that on a date certain, say, six months hence, the president will instruct the secretary of Treasury to coordinate with the Federal Reserve to stabilize the value of the dollar relative to gold, to a band of plus or minus 20 percent of the one-year moving average of the spot price of gold on that date. (The one-year period would be centered on the date of the announcement.)

- If the average spot price of gold for the last five trading days of this six-month period is below this 20 percent band (that is, less than 80 percent of its twelve-month average price), then the Federal Reserve would be required to stabilize the value of the dollar relative to gold to a band of plus or minus 20 percent centered on a price 10 percent above that five-day moving average price at the end of the twelve-month period.

- Conversely, if the average spot price of gold for the last five trading days of this six-month period is above this 20 percent band (that is, greater than 120 percent of its twelve-month average price), then the Federal Reserve would be required to stabilize the value of the dollar relative to gold to a band of plus or minus 20 percent centered on a price 10 percent below the five-day moving average price at the end of the twelve-month period.

During this six-month period, the Fed should continue to pursue policies consistent with its dual mandate and should not attempt to manipulate the price of gold.

Begin Orderly Phaseout

The president would instruct the secretary of the Treasury to consult with the Federal Reserve to phase out, through an orderly process, interest paid on excess reserves. The current interest on reserves paid by the Federal Reserve of 25 basis points is above thirty-day Treasury yields and the overnight Fed funds rate. As such, interest on reserves subsidizes bank profits and encourages banks to sit on their deposits rather than make loans.

In addition, the Fed is using these deposits to fund the purchase of longer-maturity Treasury securities and mortgage-backed securities. By so doing, it is leveraging its balance sheet by borrowing short and lending long, introducing a potential source of financial instability to the U.S. financial system.

Interest may be paid on required reserves at a rate not to exceed the overnight Fed funds rate so that banks will not be at a competitive disadvantage to the nonbanking system with regard to their vital role of intermediation between depositor and borrower.

Introduce Necessary Legislation

Introduce legislation that would restore dollar-gold convertibility and define the dollar as a unit weight of gold by following a four-step process:

Step 1: On a date certain six months after the legislation is signed into law, the secretary of the Treasury will coordinate with the Federal Reserve to further stabilize the value of the dollar relative to gold to a band of plus or minus 10 percent of the thirty-day average spot price of gold on that date. As of that date, the Fed's dual mandate would be replaced with a single mandate: to stabilize the value of the dollar within this gold band.

During this period, the Fed may target the Fed funds rate. However, in the event that the dollar approached the upper band of the gold price, the Fed would be required to suspend its interest rate target and engage directly in open-market operations by selling assets into the open market, thereby reducing the monetary base to assure that the upper band was not breached.

Conversely, if the dollar were to approach the lower band of the gold price, the Fed would be required to suspend its interest rate target and engage in open-market operations by buying Treasury bills, thereby increasing the monetary base to assure that the lower band was not breached.

Step 2: On a date certain twelve months after the legislation is signed into law, the secretary of the Treasury will coordinate with the Federal Reserve to further stabilize the value of the dollar relative to gold to a band of plus or minus 5 percent of the thirty-day average spot price of gold on that date.

During this period, the Fed would change its operating procedures to directly target the dollar's value in terms of gold and permit the Fed funds rate to be set by market forces. Instead of targeting the Fed funds rate, it would buy and sell securities only in response to movements in the value of the dollar relative to gold. In the event the dollar were to approach the upper band of the gold price, the Fed would be required to engage directly in open-market operations by selling assets into the open market, thereby reducing the monetary base to assure that the upper band was not breached.

Conversely, if the dollar were to approach the lower band of the gold price, the Fed would be required to engage in open-market operations by buying Treasury bills, thereby increasing the monetary base to assure that the lower band was not breached.

Step 3: On a date certain twenty-four months after the legislation is signed into law, the secretary of the Treasury will coordinate with the Federal Reserve to further stabilize the value of the dollar relative to gold to a band of plus or minus 2 percent of the thirty-day average spot price of gold.

During this period, the Fed would continue to directly target the dollar's value in terms of gold and permit the Fed funds rate to be set by market forces. Instead of targeting the Fed funds rate, it would buy and sell securities only in response to movements in the value of the dollar relative to gold. In the event the dollar were to approach the upper band of the gold price, the Fed would be required to engage directly in open-market operations by selling securities into the open market, thereby reducing the monetary base to assure that the upper band was not breached.

Conversely, if the dollar were to approach the lower band of the gold price, the Fed would be required to engage in open-market operations by buying Treasury bills, thereby increasing the monetary base to assure that the lower band was not breached.

Step 4: On a date certain thirty months after the legislation is signed into law the secretary of the Treasury will coordinate with the Federal Reserve to establish the value of the dollar relative to gold by setting it equal to the thirty-day average spot price of gold, rounded to the nearest $10, and to restore full dollar-gold convertibility at that price. From that point forward, the dollar would be defined as a fixed weight of gold at that exchange rate.

On that date, the U.S. government would exchange gold coins and bullion for currency and funds on deposit at the Federal Reserve on demand through any national bank at the fixed rate of exchange defined by the dollar's value as a fixed weight of gold.

The legislation would require the Fed to maintain the fixed rate of exchange between the dollar and gold by abiding by its new operating rules.

Begin International Discussions

The president would instruct the secretary of the Treasury to begin discussions with the foreign ministers and central banks of the Group of 20 major economies for the purpose of creating a 21st Century International Gold Standard that would provide a stable and secure international monetary system and promote trade and prosperity throughout the world. The goal would be to convene an international monetary conference in Washington no later than January 31, 2015, for the purpose of ratifying this new international monetary system.

The International Monetary Fund would see its role reduced to what it had been in the years following World War II, when it assisted midsized countries in establishing a fixed rate of exchange to a dollar backed in gold. Under a 21st Century Gold Standard, midsized and smaller countries would be encouraged to fix their exchange rates to any one of the key currencies at the core of the international gold standard and fully convertible into gold.

The IMF would require vastly fewer resources for this task than it currently has. Under the agreement of the international monetary conference, it would return the majority of its capital to those countries that supplied it, including the United States, and retain only what it needs for its lessened purposes.

The key features of the international gold standard are these:

1. All of the key currencies would be convertible, on demand, into a fixed weight of gold.

2. International settlements between countries would be honored in gold, or a currency convertible into gold, based on the choice of the redeeming country.

3. Central banks would be limited in their ability to sterilize gold inflows or outflows.

New Operating Rules for the Federal Reserve

First, some background on the Federal Reserve.

For the past forty years—ever since President Richard Nixon broke the final link between the dollar and gold—the Federal Reserve has attempted to create maximum employment and price stability by manipulating interest rates, the availability of credit, and the value of the dollar.

After forty years, it is clear that the Fed has failed completely to achieve either of these goals. Under the paper dollar, the U.S. economy has experienced lower growth rates, higher average unemployment, deeper and more prolonged recessions, a series of financial crises, highly volatile interest rates, an unending rise in prices, and a decline in the value of the dollar.

This failure is not the result of the skill or intelligence of the men who have chaired the Federal Reserve, nor of those men and women who have served faithfully on the Federal Reserve's Open Market Committee. The failure of the Fed is fundamentally a structural problem that requires reform of the monetary system and of the Fed's dual mandate.

First, it is not possible to hit two targets with a single arrow. One policy tool cannot achieve the two objectives of maximum employment and stable prices. As a practical matter, when these two objectives appear to come into conflict, as they do in this period, the Fed forgoes its commitment to stable prices and attempts to stimulate the economy and employment through the manipulation of interest rates and the depreciation of the dollar or, as in recent years, through a massive increase in the monetary base known as "quantitative easing."

The second, more fundamental problem is this: the premise that the Fed can maximize employment by permitting it both to manipulate interest rates, the availability of credit, and the value of our paper dollar and to print money at will is false. The experience of the past forty years, to say nothing of the entire nineteenth century, shows clearly that a dollar whose value is defined as a unit weight of gold leads to higher average economic growth rates, less severe recessions, and higher average employment.

Finally, under the post–World War II Bretton Woods system, the Fed chose to ignore the gold signal, viewing the outflow of gold as indicative of a shortage of gold instead of a surplus of dollars, ultimately leading to monetary disorder and the complete demise of the international monetary system.

As a consequence, implementation of the new gold standard requires a legislated change in the Fed's operating rules. The main principles of the new operating rules are these:

1. The Fed must guarantee the value of the dollar in terms of gold without restricting the quantity of dollars necessary to fuel real economic growth with no inflation.

2. The primary mechanism to increase or decrease the monetary base (the supply of dollars) in order to maintain the dollar's value in terms of gold will be open-market operations. The Fed will not target or manipulate short-term interest rates.

3. The United States will mint gold coins of a fixed weight and purity, which will be legal tender and circulate as money.

4. Individuals must have the right to exchange currency and deposits at the Fed for gold at a fixed price and, conversely, exchange gold coins and bullion for dollars at the same price.

5. The Fed shall not sterilize gold inflows or outflows. Instead, it shall conduct its open-market operations so that, over time, the gold stock owned by the government remains relatively unchanged.

Under this proposal, legislation would be passed to provide a gradual, clear path to establish the value of the dollar relative to gold over a period of thirty months, as outlined in "The Transition to a New Gold Standard," above. At the end of the thirty-month transition, the dollar would be defined as a fixed weight of gold.

At that point, the U.S. government would exchange, on demand, gold coins and bullion for currency and funds on deposit at the Federal Reserve, through any national bank at the fixed rate of exchange defined by the dollar's value as a fixed weight of gold or currency for gold bullion or coins at the same rate of exchange.

The legislation would require the Fed to maintain the fixed rate of exchange between the dollar and gold by adhering to the following set of operating rules:

1. The Fed would engage in open-market operations with the sole purpose of stabilizing the value of the dollar in terms of gold.

2. In the event of a gold outflow, the Fed would allow the automatic reduction in the monetary base (no sterilization).

   a. If the gold outflow equaled 1 percent or more of the U.S. gold reserves, the Fed could at its discretion further contract the monetary base by selling securities into the open market until gold flowed back into the Fed in an amount up to the outflow.

   b. If the U.S. gold reserves fell by more than 10 percent from the current level of 237 million troy ounces, the Fed would be required to sell securities from its portfolio into the open market until the outflows of gold were reversed and gold reserves were restored to a minimum of 214 million troy ounces.

3. In the event of a gold inflow, the Fed would permit the automatic increase in the monetary base (no sterilization).

   a. If the U.S. gold reserves increased by more than 1 percent, the Fed could at its discretion further expand the monetary base by purchasing securities until gold left the Fed in an amount up to the gold inflow.

b. If the gold reserves increased by more than 10 percent from the current level of 237 million troy ounces, the Fed would be required to purchase securities in the open market until the inflows of gold were reversed and gold reserves were restored to 260 million troy ounces or less.

4. The Fed would maintain its role as lender of last resort for national banks during a liquidity crisis by lending at a penalty discount rate to be set at a minimum of 1 percent above the one-year Treasury bill rate. The Fed would accept as pledges only good collateral and/or Treasury securities with maturities of one year or less.

5. The Fed would maintain its responsibilities for the regulation of bank holding companies and banks.

How the Gold Standard Works

Won't returning to a gold standard create a shortage of gold?

No. The U.S. government holds more than enough gold to sustain a dollar gold standard.

Currently, the government owns 260 million ounces of gold. At a market price of $1,700 per ounce, that is worth $442 billion, or more than 40 percent of the currency in circulation ($1,058 billion) and more than 15 percent of the $2.6 trillion monetary base.

Under the classical gold standard, gold reserves typically were less than 10 percent of currency in circulation.

What would the U.S. government have to accept in the exchange for gold?

Currency in circulation or dollars on deposit at the Federal Reserve.

How would that actually work for someone like me?

You could go to your bank and exchange currency or dollars in your checking account for a gold coin with a specific weight and fineness. Given how much the dollar has fallen in value, the smallest coin might be for $1,000.

Or you could go to your bank with a $1,000 gold coin and exchange it for $1,000 in currency or a $1,000 deposit in your checking account. Here again, it doesn't matter whether you actually decide to convert your dollars for a gold coin. The actions of a few benefit the many. As long as this exchange privilege is available to all, it constrains the politicians' ability to print money out of thin air.

That doesn't sound very practical. Who wants to walk around with a $1,000 gold coin in his pocket?

Actually, very few of us would walk around or use gold coins in our day-to-day lives. Under a gold standard, you would continue to use currency and your credit or debit cards just as you do now. But when the dollar is as good as gold, you will have the right to exchange, as in the example above, $1,000 for a specific and unchanging amount of gold or vice versa. This aspect of the gold standard gives you and all other holders of dollars the ability to hold the government accountable for the value of the dollar.

Would the U.S. government be required to hold enough gold to back, on a 1:1 basis, currency in circulation?

No. The Bank of England, which was at the center of the world gold standard for more than a hundred years, held only about 1:20 amount of gold relative to currency in circulation. Adam Smith called for a 1:5 ratio.

How would you set the price of gold?

There are four principles for an orderly return to a new gold standard:

- Overall prices should remain near today's levels, including no downward pressure on wages.

- The process for establishing the new link between the dollar and gold must be transparent—making use of markets to establish the value of the dollar in terms of gold.

- The transition must be gradual, but the path would be clear. This will permit as smooth an adjustment process as possible.

- The Fed will be given new operating procedures to ensure that under the new gold standard, the Fed will guarantee the value of the dollar and will not restrict the number of dollars available for the economy to grow.

But what if a series of individuals or governments demand gold in exchange for currency or bank deposits in the United States. Wouldn't the government eventually run out of gold?

No. The Fed could meet each exchange out of its inventory of gold. It could also sell securities from its portfolio, thereby further reducing the monetary base.

At some point, this process would create a scarcity of dollars relative to gold (at the fixed rate of exchange between the dollar and gold) such that an individual or country would present gold for either currency or dollar deposits in a bank in the United States.

What would happen if the Chinese wanted to exchange the $1 trillion we owe them for gold?

The Chinese government currently keeps its dollar holdings in Treasury securities. To convert these holdings into gold, it would have to first sell these securities in the secondary market in order to obtain balances on deposit in a U.S. bank. It could then instruct its bank to present those deposits in exchange for gold.

In such an unlikely event, in which the Chinese would surely take a considerable loss on the bond sales, the Fed could sell from its portfolio $1 trillion in securities and use the money to purchase gold at the fixed rate of exchange, which it would then deliver to the Chinese.

Note: This would cause the Fed to contract the monetary base by more than 30 percent, no doubt leading to a scarcity of dollars and an appreciation of the dollar relative to gold. That would trigger a movement by other players to exchange gold for dollars until the balance between dollars and gold was restored at the fixed rate of exchange.

In the face of truly extraordinary demand for official gold, the Federal Reserve could be permitted to meet its conversion requirements over a period of weeks.

What would keep the United States (and other governments) from breaking their commitment to a gold standard as soon as it became politically inconvenient, such as under Nixon in 1971?

There are only two vehicles to keep the U.S. government from breaking its commitment, which in turn will keep other governments from doing the same: political pressure from the voters and the Constitution.

The paper dollar has been a disaster for the American people. The idea that the Federal Reserve could manage the economy by manipulating interest rates and the value of our dollar has proven to be false. Real incomes have stagnated as the dollar has fallen in value to less than two dimes of what it could buy in 1971. Recessions have become deeper, unemployment rates higher, and financial crises endemic.

As monetary stability is restored by making the dollar as good as gold, political support will sustain it until we forget the lessons of the last forty years.

In addition, gold and silver coins would once again circulate as legal tender, making it more difficult to debase the dollar or sever the link between the dollar and gold without, as occurred in the 1930s, the seizure of all such coins by the federal government.

Eventually, it would be very beneficial to add the gold standard explicitly to the Constitution, as the founding fathers originally thought they had.

What would the role of the Fed be under a gold standard?

The Federal Reserve's primary role would be to stand ready to purchase or sell dollars at a fixed rate of exchange into gold and to manage its gold reserves.

The Fed's secondary role would be to perform the function of "lender of last resort." It would fulfill this role by maintaining its discount rate moderately above market rates and be willing to discount real bills—that is, high-quality, self-liquidating commercial paper.

The Fed would also retain its vital role as a regulator of bank holding companies and banks.

The Gold Standard and the Great Depression

Didn't the gold standard contribute to the Great Depression?

No. What we now know as the Great Depression started as a recession, similar to the recession in 1919. In both cases, we were on a gold standard, and the Fed mismanaged it. But what turned the recession of the early 1930s into the Depression was a series of additional policy errors that intensified the severity and duration of the downturn.

Right after the Fed was created in 1913, it went wild printing money, so much so that it caused 100 percent inflation over six short years.

Income tax rates that were suddenly jacked up to 77 percent did nothing to curtail the inflation. So in 1920, the Fed started to tighten massively—just as it would do later in 1930. The result was a recession. But instead of exacerbating the recession, the response from Congress and the president was totally different. Republican president Warren Harding (and later Calvin Coolidge) took the advice of his Treasury secretary, Andrew Mellon, and arranged for a series of tax cuts that would take the top rate down by two-thirds, to 25 percent. The huge investment and consumer boom of the Roaring Twenties followed. The policy mix of recommitting to gold in the context of major tax cuts freed people to use good money in the private sector. And they did in a big way.

By 1928, the Fed was so "embarrassed" by a stock market on fire that it began a five-year program where it would starve the economy of money. Then, in 1929, the stock market crashed the day after some final hurdles were cleared in Congress that made passage of the Smoot-Hawley tariffs likely. This was a massive tax increase on international trade, quadrupling the tax to 60 percent on 3,200 imported products. The economy, along with the stock market, started to go into free fall. Amazingly, Congress decided to double-down on what the money masters at the Fed were doing and threw in mammoth tax increases. In 1932, tax rates were increased across the board, with the top personal income tax rate jumping to 63 percent from 25 percent. The Fed raised interest rates, stood by while banks failed by the thousands, and hoarded its gold.

By 1933, we had a Great Depression where a quarter of the nation's workforce was unemployed and a great decade's worth of economic production and opportunity was wiped out. The new president, Franklin Roosevelt, failed to reform the Fed and only increased taxes (as well as regulations) from their new high base, so the Depression persisted all decade long.

The constant in the two episodes is the gold standard. The variable is federal intervention and the reach of tax policy. Therefore, the culprit behind the 1929–1933 event—as well as the savior of the 1919–1920 situation—resides in taxes. They went down big-time in the context of gold, and we got the Roaring Twenties. They went up big-time in the early 1930s in the context of gold, and we got the Great Depression. To associate the Great Depression with the gold standard is to make a hefty category mistake.

The moral of the story is: let the economy be! When the Fed engineered inflation from 1913 to 1919, which coincided with a huge tax increase, we experienced slow growth, then a recession. In the 1920s, when taxes were low and the Fed kept its head down, we had one of the great runs of all time. After 1929, as the Fed and the rest of the government got activist again, our economy plunged as it never had before and stayed laid low for a decade.

My campaign was privileged to have among its advisers the researchers and scholars who have broken ground on these key historical points. The great Jude Wanniski, who wrote *The Way the World Works*, started the ball rolling in the 1970s by reinterpreting the Great Depression. One of his mentees, Paul Hoffmeister, was also on my campaign. Brian Domitrovic, whose book Econoclasts described the real history of the 1920s and 1930s, joined Paul Hoffmeister and Chuck Kadlec (a protégé of the great Arthur Laffer's) to affirm my campaign's commitment to low taxes and sound, gold-based monetary policy.

Didn't going off gold in the 1930s prompt the recovery from the Great Depression?

No. The United States went off gold in 1933, and that year came in as badly as the Depression's trough year of 1932 in all the major economic categories. In 1934, the United States resumed the gold standard (if at a higher price), and the recovery got going. It was a mediocre recovery, in that going off gold and the dollar devaluation against gold had introduced a lack of clarity in the system.

The Gold Standard and the Economy

Doesn't a gold standard lead to more recessions?

Absolutely not. The classical gold standard leads to fewer, shorter, and shallower recessions.

In the nineteenth century, the noteworthy "panics," such as those of 1873 and 1893, were caused by the United States wavering in its commitment to keep the dollar as good as gold. In both cases, however, the United States came around to renewing its commitment to the gold standard, and the recoveries that came were stupendous and immediate. The run of growth from 1873 to 1892 was the greatest in American history—4.7 percent per year. From 1894 to 1913, growth was 3.6 percent, above the post-1913 average of 3.2 percent.

After World War II, the United States defined the dollar as one-thirty-fifth of an ounce of gold. This version of the gold standard was somewhat flawed, in that U.S. residents could not exchange dollars for gold coins and the ownership of gold bullion was prohibited. This kept the trump card out of the hands of the people and vested it with bureaucrats, a flaw of the Bretton Woods system that our policy doesn't repeat.

The federal government did, however, exchange gold for dollars with foreign central banks. The post–World War II period provides a useful reference point for how the U.S. economy performed when the United States last guaranteed the dollar in terms of gold.

From 1947 through 1967, the yearly average unemployment rate never rose above 6.7 percent and overall averaged less than 5 percent. By contrast, since 1971, when the United States stopped guaranteeing the dollar in terms of gold, the yearly average unemployment rate has peaked at 9.6 percent or greater three times, and averaged more than 6 percent.

If the United States went on a gold standard, wouldn't that reduce our international competitiveness?

No. First, a strong and stable dollar has been good for jobs and growth. Under the strong dollar policies of Presidents Eisenhower, Kennedy, Reagan, and Clinton, the United States experienced above-average growth in employment and output.

Second, U.S. efforts to improve our competitive position by devaluation have failed time and time again.

One of the promises made by President Nixon and the advocates of breaking the gold standard was that it would improve our competitive position by allowing us to devalue the dollar. But devaluation has not worked.

In 1967, $1 could buy 2.4 euros (based on the pre-euro German mark) and 362 yen. Since then, the dollar has been devalued by more than 70 percent against both currencies. Yet net exports have dropped from a modest surplus in 1967 to a $390 billion deficit, equivalent to 2.7 percent of GDP.

But under a gold standard, wouldn't the U.S. trade deficit grow?

Not necessarily. In general, a trade deficit reflects something far more basic than a nation's competitiveness. The trade deficit is the difference between domestic savings and investment.

The gold standard will reduce the "bad" trade deficit, which contributes to job losses. Under the current system of floating currencies, the world is on a de facto paper dollar standard. This creates an artificial demand for U.S. Treasury securities by foreign central banks and corporations.

But to increase their holdings of dollar deposits, foreign entities have to sell more goods and services in the United States than they buy in the United States, which increases the deficit on the trade account.

Under an international gold standard, gold and other gold-backed currencies would be ready substitutes for the dollar. As a consequence, foreigners would be less inclined to trade goods for Treasury bills but would seek to trade goods in exchange for imports of American-made goods or services. This would put in place powerful economic forces that would lead to a reduction in the "bad" trade and an increase in the U.S. savings rate. When these powerful economic forces are coupled with the elimination of the tax bias that ships jobs overseas, the United States will dominate world trade.

At the same time, the gold standard may increase the "good" trade deficit that leads to increased jobs and opportunities for American workers. The increased economic growth made possible by a gold standard will make the United States an even more attractive place to invest by both U.S. and foreign companies. The increase in investment relative to savings will increase the net inflow of capital, which is reflected in an increase in the trade deficit.

For example, when Toyota or Mercedes-Benz builds a new auto-manufacturing plant in the United States, it is taking the dollars it earns by selling cars in the United States and using them to purchase goods and services in the United States. But instead of exporting those goods back to Japan or Germany, it keeps them here to build a factory, leading to an increase in the trade deficit. In this case, the American economy benefits not only from the jobs created to build the factory but also from the ongoing jobs needed to operate the factory.

In either case, a gold standard is the best way to deal with a trade deficit. A major trade deficit for a country is especially worrisome if it has been caused by government borrowing abroad to finance public-sector projects, which often fail to generate enough returns to pay the interest on a country's external debt. This creates the risk that the politicians will ultimately raise taxes.

A gold standard drastically improves economic performance and encourages private investment while creating natural conditions for low interest rates. In this case, the taxpayers are not liable to repay the debt.

However, they benefit from the jobs and opportunities created by increased investment in the U.S. economy.

How will it help restrain spending?

By making it possible for the economy to grow faster, the gold standard will reduce the federal budget deficit by generating increased revenues through a larger tax base and by decreasing the need and demand for government transfer payments and other low-return spending. Deficit spending will be restrained because the government can't print gold. If it printed money anyway, ordinary holders of dollars would convert the surplus dollars to gold, thereby taking what the government prints right back out of circulation as fast as it could print it.

Wouldn't a return to the gold standard require the United States to raise interest rates to defend the dollar?

No. Under a gold standard, the U.S. government does not attempt to manage the economy or the foreign exchange value of the dollar by manipulating interest rates. Rather, it guarantees the fixed rate of exchange between the dollar and gold. There would be no need to defend the dollar or to intervene on foreign exchange markets.

But, if foreign entities have less of an incentive to buy Treasury securities under a gold standard than under the current dollar standard, won't that lead to higher interest rates?

No. In the trillion-dollar international financial markets, the Federal Reserve can have little, if any, effect on any rate other than the overnight Fed funds rate. In general, interest rates on U.S. government debt are based on investor assessments of the risk of inflation.

While the price level under a gold standard has fluctuated up and down on a year-to-year basis, over the longer term there has been no increase in prices. As a result, interest rates under a gold standard are low and stable.

For example, from 1948 to 1967 consumer price inflation in the United States averaged less than 2 percent, and interest rates on AAA corporate bonds averaged only 3.7 percent. Mortgages and consumer credit were readily available for all qualified borrowers and were far lower than the prevailing interest rates under the paper dollar.

But those interest rates are higher than today's interest rates. So wouldn't interest rates have to rise under a gold standard?

We are living through a historically anomalous period of low interest rates that will not last. Even the White House is projecting rising rates as unemployment begins to abate in the next upturn of the business cycle.

In addition, inflation has begun to accelerate to above 5 percent. Without monetary reform, rising interest rates could quickly add as much as $800 billion a year in uncontrolled federal spending by increasing interest payments on the debt to $1 trillion a year.

By contrast, when the dollar was last unquestionably convertible into gold (at least internationally) in the 1950s and early 1960s, Treasury bill yields averaged 2.2 percent, and yields on longer maturities averaged just 3.3 percent. If the rise in interest rates over the next nine years could be held to those levels, federal expenditures could be reduced by $1 trillion.

Isn't the gold standard just a top-down way for Wall Street bankers to impose austerity on the rest of the country?

To the contrary. For a number of technical reasons, Wall Street is greatly privileged by the world paper dollar standard, leading to a greater gap between rich and poor. The gold standard is the working person's friend.

Won't a gold standard put hedge fund managers in charge of U.S. monetary policy?

They are in charge of U.S. monetary policy now. Bill Clinton once famously told Robert Rubin that he wanted to be reincarnated as the bond market, which was preventing him from undertaking some programs he wished to initiate. The gold standard puts monetary policy into the hands of the people rather than elite civil servants (who are very cozy with hedge fund managers).

By reducing U.S. access to foreign lenders, wouldn't a gold standard increase the risk of a debt crisis for the United States similar to what is confronting European countries such as Greece, Ireland, Spain, and Portugal?

No. Monetary reform that includes restoring the gold standard would reduce the risk of a U.S. debt crisis. Making the dollar as good as gold (by making it convertible into gold) would make U.S. companies and the government even more secure, and therefore desirable, borrowers, and at a lower interest rate than would otherwise be possible. Think of it as the difference between a collateralized and a non-collateralized loan.

In addition, during the 1950s and 1960s, the U.S. economy grew at 4 percent a year with little inflation. A gold standard would complement the pro-growth tax reforms in the budget outline. By supporting higher rates of employment and economic growth, a gold standard would expand the tax base and thereby increase revenues to the federal government, as well as to hard-pressed state and local governments.

Won't the gold standard limit the increase in the amount of dollars to just 2 percent a year, the average annual increase in the quantity of gold?

No. The rapid economic growth and dramatic increase in the standard of living during the nineteenth-century Industrial Revolution were accomplished under a gold standard. Under a 21st Century Gold Standard, the Federal Reserve would be required to maintain the value of the dollar in terms of gold and exchange gold coins and bullion for currency or deposits at the Fed. For the most part, this would be accomplished through open-market operations, with the 260 million ounces of gold currently owned by the government acting as a buffer stock. There would be no requirement to increase this stockpile of gold in order to increase the amount of dollars in circulation.

The key point is that under the 21st Century Gold Standard, the Fed is required to guarantee the quality or value of the dollar. As long as the value of the dollar is constant in terms of gold, the Federal Reserve would be able to provide all the money the economy needs to fuel real economic growth without inflation.

Why not define the dollar in terms of a basket of commodities?

Gold itself is the best indication of the average price of all commodities. Coming up with a basket would be redundant and invite shenanigans. Currently, the government's consumer price index is a "basket" of goods and services, and that basket has been manipulated for political purposes over the years.

Why target the price of gold? Why not just repeal the "maximum employment" part of the Fed's dual mandate, leaving a single mandate to stabilize the price level?

The only pressure on the Fed in this case would come from its mandate. That's not enough. The problem is that the notion of stable prices is ill defined and therefore can easily be manipulated by the Federal Reserve to suit its desire to manipulate interest rates and the value of our dollar. By contrast, defining the dollar as a unit weight of gold is an explicit promise that cannot be fudged. In addition, the ability of individuals to redeem currency or deposits in their checking account for gold is an important check on the power of the government to debase the value of the dollar.

Why does the path to a gold standard take thirty months?

It provides for a gradual but clear path toward making the dollar as good as gold, which will make the adjustment process as smooth as possible. Gold would be targeted gradually, but ever more firmly with every passing month, so that by the expiration of the president's term the dollar would be defined as a fixed weight of gold. The current price of gold may be ill suited to serve as the conversion price since it may reflect a speculative hedge against future inflation. The thirty-month discovery process will allow market forces to find the price of gold consistent with today's price level.

Why is the initial band plus or minus 20 percent?

Historically (for example, in the 1980s), when there are tax cuts that bring money out of hiding and into productive uses in the real economy, gold falls and then proceeds forward in a 20 percent band for a time. With 9-9-9, we can expect a similar pattern. But unlike in the 1980s, after 2012, with a path to gold convertibility made explicit, we can expect the band of oscillation of gold to narrow.

Why use a moving average price at the end of each of the price targets during the transition to gold?

Gold can fluctuate day to day. Moving averages will average out these fluctuations into one number.

Why forbid the Fed to target interest rates?

Interest rates are a market price between lenders and borrowers of money that is best left to the market to decide.

How can the United States be the only country on a gold standard? If all other countries peg their currencies to the dollar (but not to gold), won't that create the same kind of trade tensions as we now have with China?

We have trade tensions with China now because we are not on the gold standard.

It is highly unlikely the United States will be the only country on a gold standard. In fact, announcing its intention to restore the dollar to the gold standard positions the United States to lead the world toward a far more stable international monetary system than we have today with gyrating currencies.

The world's major countries will find it in their self-interest to link their currencies directly to gold, as opposed to linking it to gold through a link to the dollar as they did under Bretton Woods. First, having only one currency convertible into gold, as under Bretton Woods, proved to be unstable. Therefore, a system where multiple currencies are convertible into gold is more stable. Second, if a country's currency is convertible into gold, then it is more likely to be able to conduct trade in its currency, as opposed to the dollar.

We would expect major currencies, including the euro, British pound, Chinese yuan, and Japanese yen, to link directly to gold. Other major countries, including Canada, India, and Brazil, would also be invited to join the group of gold-backed currencies.

If the dollar were the only currency convertible into gold, wouldn't such an asymmetric system lead to an overvalued dollar and encourage deficit spending on the part of the federal government (by creating a demand for U.S. Treasury securities)?

The gold standard will create demand for currency to be used in the real economy. The booms will come not in inert investments like Treasury securities but in businesses and entrepreneurial ventures now free to run on account of a stable means of exchange.

Chapter 9

Energy Independence and Security

Failure is the opportunity to begin again more intelligently.

—Henry Ford

Red, White, and Blue Energy

As this book goes to print, the price of gasoline is pushing $4 a gallon in most of the country. Depending on the size of your state gasoline taxes, it may already be above that—or in some cases well above that.

Momentary high gas prices, of course, represent only one of the problems we face when we depend so heavily on other nations to supply us with oil. It's a problem that has vexed presidents for several generations, while the nation found itself all too often at the mercy of sheikhs, emirs, princes, and potentates who decide what to produce, how much to produce, and what we will pay for it.

If ever a situation cried out for a change of plans, this is it.

Drill here, drill now, we often hear. Yes! We should! But do you ever wonder why we don't?

Part of the reason is stupid federal regulations and moratoriums. We all know that. But even if those were lifted tomorrow, there are problems with our tax code and our monetary policies that would make it difficult to accomplish complete energy independence and security.

This is what the Solutions Revolution is all about: 9-9-9, a Regulatory Budget Office, and a 21st Century Gold Standard equal energy independence and security.

May I introduce a new term into the energy dialogue? I would like to begin transitioning from energy "independence" to energy "security." Until now, the two have been used interchangeably. In fact, while on the campaign trail, I saw that the words "energy independence" get an applause everywhere in America. However, energy independence means no imported energy at all. We wouldn't want that. Trade is good, especially trade with friends, and our neighbors, Canada and Mexico, represent over 40 percent of our oil imports. The real goal should be (1) that our energy needs are supplied from secure sources, and (2) that we do not pursue tax, regulatory, or monetary policies that artificially push prices higher and result in a transfer of wealth from Americans to oil-producing nations that are hostile to U.S. interests. Using this definition, energy security is more appropriate than energy independence. The independence we seek is not from all foreign sources but from hostile sources. This implies security. Since some habits are harder to change than others, I won't hold it against you if you still applaud "energy independence" as long as you don't hold it against me that I sometimes still use the term myself.

We can achieve energy security, but you would never know it to listen to President Obama. We are in the middle of an American energy renaissance. Let's not kill it with bad tax, regulatory, and monetary policies.

The president clearly dreams of a day when we all live completely and totally on alternative, renewable energy sources. His latest push is seaweed. And there is nothing wrong with any of these energy sources once they can be made technologically and economically viable. But the president acts as though strength and independence with respect to oil were somehow a bad thing—like improving our ability to produce our own fossil fuels. This kind of thinking ends all possibility of developing new energy concepts.

That's stupid! Smart countries make good use of the resources they have while pursuing innovative new concepts. They don't create false either-or choices.

I wish I had a nickel for every time he said, "We represent 25 percent of oil consumption yet account for only 2 percent of oil reserves." This is clever mixing of apples and oranges. I refuse to believe his Ivy League education didn't teach him better, so I must assume it is a community organizer trick designed to mislead people.

The thing that matters is the number of barrels (or equivalent) we consume, the number of barrels (or equivalent) we produce domestically and import from friendly nations, and the number of years' supply we have available. That creates a time frame under which we can develop the technological breakthroughs to make alternative fuels more competitive. The president derives his "2 percent" from U.S. "proven reserves," about 20 billion barrels of oil. Proven reserves are the quantity of energy sources estimated with reasonable certainty, from the analysis of geologic and engineering data, to be recoverable from well-established or known reservoirs with the existing equipment and under the existing operating conditions.

Let me interpret that. It is yesterday's estimate, using yesterday's data and technology, and applying yesterday's know-how. That is so yesterday! Obama is living in the past. It misses the march of technology, the irrepressibility of entrepreneurial ingenuity, and the American spirit itself. We are always looking for new and better ways to do everything in this country. "Proven reserves" is only relevant if we use yesterday's technology forever. The United States was said to have 30 billion barrels of "proven reserves" in 1980. Yet from 1980 to 2008, we produced about 75 billion barrels of oil. No one thinks the proven reserves numbers come anywhere close to capturing our real oil resources—not even the U.S. government. The Energy Department estimated in 2006 that there were about 400 billion barrels of technically recoverable oil, including undiscovered resources, and that does not even include oil shale, which is more than a trillion barrels.[36]

Total estimated resources exceed 1.4 trillion barrels of oil in the United States, and some analysts (Goldman Sachs, Citigroup) predict that the United States has the potential to be the world's largest oil-producing country by 2017. The number the president is using, about 20 billion barrels, is less than the current best estimate for the Bakken formation in North Dakota alone.

The president's claim that "we use 25 percent of the world's oil" is false and evasive. We consume 25 percent of the world's oil production, not 25 percent of the world's oil reserves, as the president's comparison suggests. The president is just cherry-picking numbers. He tries to confuse us by mixing a "flow" variable such as annual consumption-production and a "stock" variable such as reserves. Does it tell you anything if I say my 401(k) contribution is 25 percent of my income but only 2 percent of my 401(k) balance? The 2 and the 25 are not meaningfully related, so the comparison makes no sense; it certainly doesn't prove we're consuming too much or that there is too little to go around.

Obama's misleading claims don't capture the fact that our domestic reserves keep increasing the more technology improves and the more capital is invested. What about his claims that domestic oil production has increased to record highs on his watch? Another clever deception. It has happened on private land, where he can't stop it; otherwise he would. And since he can't stop it, I guess he figures he should take credit for it.

We have years and years of abundant resources that we could rely on while we let the market develop alternatives. The economic environment created by the Solutions Revolution will encourage development of our own abundant resources, and make them cleaner, while investing the capital to develop competitive alternatives.

The United States currently has 20.6 billion barrels of proven oil reserves, with a consumption rate of 19 million barrels a day (6.9 billion barrels a year). Nonproven, recoverable oil resources are estimated at 116 billion barrels but could be much higher considering that substantial federal lands are currently off-limits for exploration and have not been fully evaluated.

President Obama has blocked drilling in offshore areas totaling more than ten times the size of Texas. He has stalled progress on an estimated 1 trillion barrels of oil in the American West, where the federal government owns the majority of the world's oil shale. These off-limits supplies alone give the United States some of the largest oil reserves in the world.

Domestic proven natural gas reserves stand at 284 trillion cubic feet. There is an estimated total of up to 3,000 trillion cubic feet of probable and possible recoverable reserves. The United States consumed 24.62 trillion cubic feet in 2010, implying a supply in excess of one hundred years.

Over the last five years, a dramatic increase in recoverable oil and gas reserves has been made possible by the advances in horizontal drilling and hydraulic fracture stimulation ("fracking") technologies. None of these new technologies was developed with government subsidies or mandates. (Note: Another myth is that big oil companies receive a lot of taxpayer subsidies. Nonsense. They deduct the cost of goods sold, depreciation, and depletion, just like every other business. When a community organizer has an agenda, these basic accounting deductions are turned into "taxpayer subsidies" to cover up the lavish real subsidies given to his cronies like solar company Solyndra.) While there has been concern about groundwater contamination from fracking, in the more than 1 million wells completed with proper fracking techniques, there has not been a confirmed case of groundwater contamination.

It is a fracking lie told by fracking environmental extremists to stop our fracking entrepreneurs from developing our fracking resources. That is fracking nonsense!

The United States has been blessed with massive coal reserves. Estimates suggest there are literally hundreds of years of coal reserves to be mined, for domestic use or export, further suggesting that the potential exists to create meaningful employment for hundreds of thousands of Americans for many years.

The process is getting cleaner too, and not because of government. We have been steadily reducing our carbon emissions relative to the size of the economy from the days when wood was the primary fuel. Markets and competition always look to do more with less. Without the heavy hand of government, the market moved to coal, then crude oil, now natural gas. In the future it could be any number of sources.

What drives the adoption of new technology? It isn't the fist of government punishing today's most economically viable fuels. Locking in inferior technology is a waste of valuable resources. What if we subsidized one of the earliest of Edison's lightbulb experiments? We might not ever have had the real thing, and it would have been a waste to subsidize a failure. Think back to when computers were made of vacuum tubes. I have a master's degree in computer science, and that time seems like yesterday. What if we had let government take control of the industry back then, on the basis of some "scientific evidence" that was never really debated? If it had, it would have been likely to publish as "scientific research" projections made by some but not subject to dispute by others that by the year 2012 computers would require so many vacuum tubes they would take up the size of a football field. And because of space constraints, the ideologues would have used their ideology to distort markets. Given that attitude, the government would have halted competition and the very innovation that led to a much preferable outcome. What a disaster. What happened instead? The market looked to do more with less, and with capital investment, risk-taking, and, most important, no government control we now have amazingly fast computing over a global wireless system on devices that fit in our hands. No bureaucrat would have predicted it (although Al Gore claims he invented it). Although a Defense Department agency invented the Internet for national security purposes, only when private markets developed it did it flourish to become the global communications system we are now experiencing.

We need to look at alternative fuels from a capital investment standpoint, not a government mandate approach. How many technological breakthroughs do we need to make seaweed competitive? I am in favor of finding out. What about wind, solar, and the other favorites? Nobody would have guessed that the materials that vaulted the computer age from vacuum tubes to what we have today were technological advances involving, of all things, sand. Abundant sand has properties that enhanced silicon's ability to speed up computing times. Sand is also used in glass, which in purified form is made into fiber-optic cables, creating the information superhighway.

But this wasn't a top-down process. Imagine any bureaucrat (besides Al Gore) saying, "I've got an idea: we will go from vacuum tubes to global wireless computing at the speed of light by researching sand." It was a diffused, bottom-up approach. One research project gives another person an idea, which prompts an entrepreneur to take a risk using it to meet a need. One entrepreneur's product spurs other entrepreneurs into building upon it. And so on. This is how innovation happens, if we allow it.

With stronger capital formation, zero capital gains tax, and expensing of business investment, we may only be a breakthrough or two away from making some of these other fuels competitive. We just need to allow entrepreneurs to take risks. Everyone knows the potential payoff if a renewable fuel can become cost competitive. The trial-and-error process is the best teacher and inevitably leads to better solutions, but only by allowing failure. Bailouts and subsidies retard progress. Government distortion will prevent us from ever achieving competitive renewable energy sources. If we subsidize windmills at outrageous rates, what incentive is there to invest in the technological breakthrough that will make them competitive?

Renewables actually get 49 times the subsidies per unit of energy produced, compared with the subsidies made to traditional sources of energy. Traditional subsidies work out to be 4 cents per BTU compared with $1.97 per BTU given to renewable sources.[37]

Did you know that at current market rates, it will take windmills seventy-five years just to break even? But they are made of materials that give them a twenty-five-year life? Instead of subsidizing them, we should incentivize entrepreneurs to find the next breakthrough that makes them and other alternative sources competitive. But isn't a subsidy a form of incentive? Yes, but it's a bad one. Investment should be made by private capital, not taxpayers' money. That way, the taxpayers have no downside, only upside.

Basically, there are two types of energy, and only two. There is energy that is worth more than it costs, and there is energy that costs more than it's worth. It's common sense. But Obama's energy strategy is to tax the former in order to subsidize the latter. We are naturally endowed with hundreds of years of oil, natural gas, and coal, all of which are worth more than they cost. We should tap this abundance. It is not a permanent condition that most alternative forms of energy cost more than they are worth. With enough investment we will get the breakthroughs to drive their value above their cost, putting them in the former category.

Lately, President Obama has been complaining that those who criticize his subsidies of alternative energy companies are "naysayers."

No, not so. We are people who want to see things done right. I'm all for alternative energy. The more sources, the better. And I want to see economic policies that encourage them to be developed in an effective way. Obama's policies don't do that.

It doesn't make sense to force the adoption of a technology that is not competitive, and by doing so harm the very process of capital investment that will produce the discovery necessary to lead to the faster adoption of alternative energy. That is stupid. 9-9-9 eliminates the special tax loopholes and credits that halt the innovations that will make alternatives competitive.

It doesn't cost the government any money to get out of the way. Private investors risk private capital, not taxpayer money. If their investment is lost, it doesn't cost the government anything, and failure gets us a step closer to the next success. If it is successful, and entrepreneurs make a bundle, the government basically has a 9 percent override on everything that happens in the economy. It will share in the success.

We need to create an environment most conducive to the entrepreneurial spirit, which is the American spirit. We will solve our energy needs if the government will allow it. Slogans like "Drill Here, Drill Now" and "Drill, Baby, Drill" say what we should do. Mine are solutions that give each the tools that focus on how to achieve energy independence and security.

Capital investment will drive breakthroughs that will make alternative fuel competitive and traditional energy cleaner. While campaigning, I met some amazing entrepreneurs who had the technology to convert coal into gas through a process called gasification. The result was zero-emission, clean-burning energy for electricity generation because the processing facility eliminated the pollutants normally associated with traditional coal-burning plants.

Will this work? I'm not sure, but I have no idea why the government won't get out of the way and let entrepreneurs try. Let them succeed or fail. I hope these guys succeed and make a bundle, as long as it is market forces that determine winners or losers.

9-9-9, Regulatory Certainty, and Sound Money Equal Energy Security

When I asked what is holding these entrepreneurs back, of course the EPA was top on their list. This is an incredibly capital-intensive process, with each plant costing several billion dollars. With increased capital formation and stronger incentives to invest capital, 9-9-9 addresses one part of the equation. Another part of the equation is addressed by the Regulatory Budget Office, which restrains the regulatory bureaucrats. Without their interference, we could change a regulation here, speed up a turnaround time there. But unless we overhaul the process, the weed will just grow back. Today investors will not put up the first dollar of investment in these kinds of new projects, despite the potential, so long as the EPA is on the loose.

The last piece of the equation is sound money. Let's say investors must put up $3 billion to $4 billion today, and the first unit of energy will not be generated for several years. Even if oil prices average $90 (assume oil is a benchmark for all energy), and that is sufficient to provide a satisfactory return, what happens if we go through the volatility of the past few years and hit a period where prices are $60 to $70? This trough in prices may not persist, but it could last long enough to push a project into bankruptcy, which not only hurts that project but casts a cloud over future ones as well. Investors react to this by investing less capital or requiring a higher rate of return to compensate for such risk. Both actions lead to less investment.

Other entrepreneurs have plans to refine abundant natural gas into diesel fuel. If they are successful, much of our transportation fleet and infrastructure could be powered by diesel refined from natural gas instead of crude oil. Might that reduce imported oil from hostile nations? Of course it would. Will it work? I'm not sure, but I have no idea why we're not even trying. We should proclaim, "Let there be risk-taking!" If entrepreneurs succeed and make real money, do you see yourself getting hurt? We all win. We all benefit—whereas the Solyndra scandal cost taxpayers $500 million. And for those of you who are quick to point out that Solyndra's loan process was initiated during the Bush administration, you'll find no rebuttal from me. The mistakes of progressives are not limited to one party, but populate them both.

And the government always wins when the private sector succeeds. Under 9-9-9, it will have a 9 percent "commission" on all successful production, on all income as it is paid to capital and labor, and all consumption. Let the goose lay some golden eggs, for crying out loud! It is common sense!

9-9-9 also levels the international trade playing field. This means we can export more of our most abundant energy, such as coal and natural gas. There will be massive investments in new infrastructure to process coal and natural gas, as mentioned above, but also new facilities to transport energy for export. 9-9-9 will make us once again the manufacturing center of the world. New energy-related manufacturing jobs will be created in steel production, onshore and offshore drilling rigs and equipment, service boats, pumping equipment for oil and gas, pipelines, oil-refining and natural-gas-processing equipment, liquefied natural gas plants, port facilities, and new railway lines for handling coal exports. Of course, certain associated industries will need to ramp up to meet the demands of an energy industry expansion, such as engineering and science jobs needed to design, model, improve, and develop old and new forms of energy production. Likewise, imported fuel will pay the business tax so it is on an equal playing field with domestic energy. This will shift additional demand to domestic sources, and shift foreign investment here, further reinforcing the need for capital investment, a restrained regulatory bureaucracy, and a stable unit of measure, the dollar.

All this in exchange for the government merely getting out of the way.

The greater capital investment under 9-9-9 will go hand in hand with sound money because the 21st Century Gold Standard will lead to lower energy prices. The best way to reduce break-even points so our energy industry is as profitable, even at lower prices, is through capital investment. As we'll see in Chapter 10, our energy independence and security are joined at the hip with national security. Sound money, less regulation, and low taxes on capital formation and production are the foundation of each. We don't buy oil from Iran, but because oil is a worldwide fungible product, we don't have to buy oil from Iran to help enrich the mad mullahs. Our failure to increase the supply of oil at home, coupled with our weak currency, enriches the mullahs just the same.

The Solutions Revolution will provide the tools to convert our red, white, and blue energy into a gusher of prosperity.

Affordability: Cheap energy is not a birthright but the result of technology and investment in and by the free market.

Responsibility: American ingenuity can bring about efficient, environmentally responsible, effective value-for-money energy solutions. We need to foster and facilitate this ingenuity, not punish it.

Security: Securing the energy future of America means equipping and supporting the energy industry, and associated businesses, with a tax, a regulatory and monetary policy framework that is compatible with the natural resources we have and with the challenges of the twenty-first century. Putting the United States on a path to energy independence and security strengthens our national security too.

Chapter 10

Peace Through Strength and Clarity

> *Of the four wars in my lifetime, none came about because the United States was too strong.*
>
> *—Ronald Reagan*

Economic Policy: The Weapon That Helped Win the Cold War

It's darkly fitting that al Qaeda chose the World Trade Center as one of its targets on 9/11. As such a strong symbol of American financial prowess, the twin towers represented the single greatest threat to the nation's enemies.

When the United States flexes its full economic power, no enemy of any kind can stand up against it. I would tell you to ask the Soviet Union, but you can't do that: the Soviet Union no longer exists. And as long as the United States embraces strong economic policies, it will have more than enough strength to prevent any liberty-hating force from gaining advantage in the global arena.

The question is whether we will embrace such policies.

In 2009, economist Paul Hoffmeister made a presentation to intelligence analysts from the CIA, the Department of Defense, and the U.S. Navy on the relationship between current monetary policy and the war against al Qaeda.[38] Two months after this presentation, Defense ran its first war games with the only weapon being "monetary policy."

Hoffmeister makes a compelling case that economic policy underpins our national security. I couldn't agree more. That's why he was chosen as one of my economic advisers for my presidential campaign.

He shows that bad U.S. economic policy directly contributed to the rise of the Soviet Union and helped fund its expansion. The period of aggressive Soviet expansion from 1971 to 1980 coincides with the closing down of the gold standard and the subsequent weakening of the dollar. The inflationary policies of the United States generated surplus cash flow for commodity-producing countries like the Soviet Union, while harming our domestic economy. When these policies were coupled with a projection of American weakness, the Soviet Union expanded. During this period, it moved into Africa, Central and South America, and South Asia, climaxing with the invasion of Afghanistan and fueling real concern about outflanking the United States in the Persian Gulf.

The Soviet leader, Leonid Brezhnev, proclaimed the Brezhnev doctrine, under which the advance of communism was deemed to be irreversible. President Reagan responded by launching a massive arms buildup, but none of the weapons he procured were ever used against the U.S.S.R. By stabilizing and strengthening the U.S. dollar, Reagan sent oil prices tumbling in real terms, thus crashing Soviet hard currency earnings and breaking the back of the Soviet economy.

According to another of my economic advisers, Louis Woodhill:

In January 1971, during the last days of the Bretton Woods gold standard, the free market gold price was $37.88/oz and crude oil was selling for $3.56/bbl [per barrel]. Adjusted via the GDP deflator, $3.56/bbl in 1971 dollars amounts to $16.02/bbl in 2011 dollars.

By the time that the Soviets invaded Afghanistan, in April 1979, gold was trading at $239.36/oz and real ($2011) crude oil prices had risen to $41.34/bbl. Real Soviet oil export earnings per barrel had increased by 158 percent from 1971 with no effort on their part.[39]

Because of Reagan's economic policies, which strengthened the dollar, "by March 1986, real crude oil prices had declined to $22.85/bbl, and Mikhail Gorbachev knew he was in trouble. The USSR had lost 73% of its oil export income in real terms."

As Woodhill further reports:

Four more years of low real crude oil prices brought the Soviet regime to the brink of bankruptcy. In May 1990, Gorbachev called German chancellor Helmut Kohl and begged him for a loan of 20 billion deutsche marks to stave off financial disaster. Kohl advanced only 5 billion deutsche marks (DM). By August 1990, Gorbachev was back, pleading for more loans. In December 1991, the Soviet Union collapsed.

Ironically, according to Hoffmeister, it was the volatility of oil prices, which caused rapidly rising prices in the 1970s, followed by falling commodity prices in the 1980s, that may have harmed the Soviets the most.[40] For as difficult as that period was for our economy, our market forces were able to adjust much more efficiently than those of the U.S.S.R.'s central planners. By Reagan's second term, our economy was exceptionally strong while the Soviets' economy was collapsing. At that point, we simply outgrew them.

Thus there is considerable geopolitical leverage to our own economic policies. Bad policy not only hurt us but strengthened our enemy. Good policy not only helped us but helped to defeat our enemy.

Economic Policy: The Weapon That Can Help Win the War on Terror

Hoffmeister applies the same principles to our global war on terror. He considers the cold war to be World War III, and therefore calls the global war on terror World War IV.

To help us prevail in World War IV, we must use sound economics that simultaneously strengthens us while weakening our enemy. But first, it is important to understand how our enemy operates. Al Qaeda operates largely outside of the global financial system. They have created their own financial network called hawalas, an ancient and rather efficient system of money exchange based on a network of money brokers. To transfer money around the globe, a person might approach a local hawaladar who calls or e-mails a counterpart overseas. The overseas hawaladar transfers cash to the intended recipient, then settles up weekly or monthly with the U.S. counterpart. Interestingly, their financial records are kept in terms of gold, so dollars, rupees, etc. would be denominated in ounces of gold. They thus keep financial assets and obligations in real terms and are shielded from the volatility and loss of purchasing power of currencies. The system is off the radar of the traditional financial system, lacks bureaucracy or a paper trail, and evades taxation. This allows terrorists and criminal elements to keep their wealth in commodities and circumvent the banking system.[41]

When the price of gold rises, al Qaeda's purchasing power increases. With the election of 2006, Democrats won control of Congress; since then, gold has risen from roughly $600 to its present level of roughly $1,700. Thus, we have enriched the very enemy we are trying to defeat by nearly threefold. At the same time, our purchasing power is being reduced since gold eventually pulls other commodity prices along, as we're seeing with oil prices.

While nobody really knows the size of al Qaeda's bankroll, this is a substantial transfer of wealth from ordinary Americans to an enemy whose cost to perpetrate the 9/11 attacks has been estimated to be as little as $500,000.

Here's how Hoffmeister sees the connection between the

combination of 9-9-9, the Regulatory Budget Office, the 21st Century Gold Standard (the three key elements of the Solutions Revolution), and our national security.

1. The resultant economic growth would create a global prosperity that would have millions to billions of future potential terrorists choose careers as opposed to murder.

2. The initial collapse and ultimate stabilization in oil prices would eliminate the petrodollars funding the current Venezuelan and Iranian governments.

3. The stabilization in gold and diamond prices would eliminate the financial advantage that al Qaeda, Hezbollah, and other terrorist organizations have that enrich them during times of geopolitical instability in a floating-dollar world. For example, the root cause of the 2008–2009 financial crisis was our floating monetary regime. The bottom line is that terrorist organizations have created a fixed monetary regime to operate within, against the floating regime in which we operate.[42]

Woodhill believes the best way to topple Hugo Chávez and Mahmoud Ahmadinejad is to stabilize the dollar.[43] Ahmadinejad's Iran is moving its uranium enrichment centrifuges underground to protect its atomic bomb program from attack. Under the leadership of Vladimir Putin, Russia has announced a $635 billion rearmament program, saying that it intends to buy 600 new planes, 1,000 new helicopters, and 100 new ships over the next ten years. Venezuela is fomenting Chávez's Bolivarian revolution throughout Latin America.

How can we counter these threats to our national security? Before we send in the Marines, we might consider stabilizing the dollar. Agreeing with Hoffmeister that the strong dollar was one of the principal weapons that Ronald Reagan used in the 1980s to topple the Soviet Union, Woodhill advises that we lead with the one weapon that has no casualties—sound monetary policy. If it worked against the much more formidable Soviet Union, we have every reason to use it today. Besides containing our enemies, it is the key to a return to our prosperity, a win-win if there ever was one.

At the time this book went to press, gold was selling for $1,655 an ounce. Crude oil was trading at $107 a barrel, which, in real terms, is almost the same as when Reagan took office. At present, an ounce of gold will buy about 15.5 barrels of crude oil, which is equal to the average of the last forty years. (See Fig. 7-8.)

With our 21st Century Gold Standard, the Fed would be required, once fully implemented, to conduct open-market operations to stabilize the value of the dollar rather than manipulate interest rates. Current gold and oil prices reflect inflation that is expected and feared, not just inflation that has already occurred. Once the gold standard is passed, gold prices would plummet, taking crude oil prices with them. Who would want to hold gold if the dollar was as good as gold?

Our policy is based on outlining in advance the transition steps that will occur on certain dates to hasten the market's ability to discover the real price of gold consistent with today's price level. This "shakes the tree" and gets the speculative component out of the gold price. From there, at predetermined dates announced in advance, the Fed must conduct open-market operations to keep gold in a gradually narrowing band until we reach a market price that is consistent with neither inflation nor deflation.

Woodhill offers several estimates of where this price for gold may end up, but one theory is it could get as low as $532 an ounce. It doesn't matter what the target gold price turns out to be, but let's go with his number.

If so, according to Woodhill,

> *Stabilizing the price of gold at $532/oz would stabilize the value of the dollar at 0.001879699 ounces of gold. Based upon the historical relationship between gold prices and crude oil prices, we could then expect crude oil to settle at around $35.50/bbl. This would, among other things, reduce the price of retail*

gasoline to well below $2.00 per gallon.

A crude oil price of $35.50/bbl would cut the oil export earnings of countries like Iran, Russia, and Venezuela by about 57 percent from where they are today. This would quickly put a damper on their ability to cause trouble. Over time, it could even bring regime change, as it did in the case of the Soviet Union.[44]

Will prices get that low? It is possible, but the point is they can and should be much lower than they are now. With such volatile oil prices, suffocating regulations, untapped domestic resources, and constrained capital investment, we do not really know what our industry break-even point is, let alone the true market price for oil. With the reforms of the Solutions Revolution, the stable oil prices, contained regulators, increased capital formation, and incentives to invest capital, as well as the opening up of our domestic resources, we may find our break-even levels to be much lower than they are today too.

To have a stable economy and stable financial markets, we must have a stable dollar. A stable dollar is also required for fast economic growth, full employment, and true prosperity. It is a bonus that something that would be so good for America would also be so bad for our adversaries.

Chapter 11

The Solutions Revolution

If there must be trouble, let it be in my day, that my child may have peace.

—*Thomas Paine*

You have more power than you realize. I understand how things appear in America right now. The political class has its agenda, and regardless of what the people want, the political class always seems to find a way to advance that agenda.

The passage of Obamacare appears to be a perfect example. Everyone knew that most people did not want this law, but the Democrats were determined to pass it, and with cover from the media they did. The voters massacred the law's backers at the polls the next chance they got, but the battle still goes on. And in one form or another—whether the Supreme Court overturns it or not, in whole or in part—the battle will continue. Health-care reform is needed, but the kind of reform matters. If you believe Obama's people, it's his way or the highway, but an Army of Davids is saying, "No way! We're gonna bring this monster down!"

Do the people really have no power in this country? Can the progressives in the political class never be held accountable? Not at all! History shows that when truly mobilized and determined, We the People get results and prevail.

Let me remind you of an example you may have forgotten. In 1989, Congress decided to give itself a 50 percent pay increase. This was done in the usual slippery way: an independent commission recommended the pay increase, which would take effect automatically unless Congress voted it down. All Congress had to do was nothing, and it would get its 50 percent increase while claiming it was someone else's idea.

Naturally, the intention of then House Speaker Jim Wright (D-Texas) was to do nothing.

In 1989, there was no Internet to speak of, but talk radio was just beginning to rise as a force in politics. The congressional pay raise caught the attention of a morning talk show host named Roy Fox on WXYT-AM in Detroit. The more Fox talked about the issue, the more incensed his listeners and callers became. Before long, Fox enlisted a network of hosts in other cities to take up the cause.

Eventually, the radio-fueled indignation grew into what became known, ironically, as the Tea Bag revolution. Invoking the spirit of the Boston Tea Party, listeners across the nation began sending tea bags to their members of Congress—demanding that they take action and vote down the pay raise.

As members of Congress felt the heat, some of them took to the floor of the House and demanded that Speaker Wright schedule the vote. Whether they were doing so out of sincerity or just to deflect the heat from their constituents, it really made no difference. They heard the voice of the people, and they knew they couldn't ignore it.

At first, Wright refused to schedule the vote, despite growing pleas from House members. But the pressure only intensified, and eventually he had no choice but to relent. The House voted down the pay raise recommendation. We the People had prevailed.

The Tea Bag revolution of 1989 succeeded because the people were well organized, well informed, and relentless. They knew what they wanted, and they would not take no for an answer. Under those circumstances, even a Congress completely indifferent to the wishes of the people had no choice but to comply.

If We the People could be so effective in a situation like this—and remember, this was before the Internet was even a factor—how is it possible that the federal government has been able to ignore the wishes of the people in so many other ways?

The answer is simple: The people cannot hold the government accountable only when it steps so far out of line that they burn with anger. They have to do it all the time. And it can't just be on hot-button issues like congressional pay. They have to do it on essential matters of policy.

But in order to do that, the people have to be well informed and truly understand the issues and the stakes. The people are at a disadvantage here because those who are supposed to keep them truly informed—the mainstream media—misinform them instead.

Indeed, they do worse than that. Does anyone remember when my friend Samuel Wurzelbacher (that's Joe the Plumber) confronted Barack Obama in 2008 and challenged his economic proposals? The media launched into a full-scale investigation—not of Obama's proposals, but of Joe! They treated a citizen who spoke truth to power as if he were a traitor to the republic.

When the political class and the media hold the people in contempt—and make no mistake, they do—it puts the people at a disadvantage in terms of both receiving information and making their voices heard.

But the advance of technology works to our advantage, just as the rise of talk radio empowered the people in 1989. It is no longer necessary to rely on establishment media to learn the facts. But there has to be a well-organized and relentless effort to keep the people informed and empowered to take action.

This nation has reached a critical point on the matter of debt, deficits, and federal spending. Last year, the national debt exceeded GDP. That's right; our debt is now bigger than the size of our entire economy. When you add in unfunded entitlement obligations, our debt-to-GDP ratio is worse than that of Greece—and you all know how much trouble Greece is in.

Under circumstances like these, you would think that members of Congress would be under massive pressure to reform entitlement programs. You would think they'd be risking political obsolescence if they don't reform Social Security, Medicare, and Medicaid immediately. And yet the opposite is true. The politicians fear political ruin if they do reform entitlements, not if they don't.

How is that possible? It is possible because those with a vested interest in the status quo have bigger megaphones and more influence on Capitol Hill. It is also possible because the average citizen has been prevented from understanding the facts. Most members of Congress do not level with the people about how serious the situation is, or about how it happened. The mainstream media are steeped in "Washington think" and do not report what the people really need to know.

That is what the Cain Solutions Revolution is going to change. We are going to make sure we understand the facts and understand the solutions. We are also going to provide the framework and the strategy for the people to demand real solutions from Congress and the White House—regardless of who controls either—just as we did in 1989, and in 1776 for that matter.

But make no mistake: it will take an Army of Davids to make this happen. This is one of the principles of good leadership I discussed earlier in the book. The CEO doesn't solve problems. The people on the ground solve problems. The CEO inspires and empowers the people to act. And there has never been a more crucial time for the people to do so.

Our great country is at a fork in the road. While the future is always uncertain, our destiny is clear. Do we continue down the path of spending, borrowing, and taxing until we steal from our children and grandchildren the opportunity that is rightfully theirs? This may be the only election we have left to change course and return to prosperity. History is full of great countries and civilizations that have collapsed. They have one thing in common—leaders who, through arrogance, lie, cheat, and steal from the people.

We are different. We are exceptional. And we must act like it. We get our rights from God Almighty, not a king or a ruler or a president who acts like a ruler. Our founders have vested in us the ability to take our power back anytime we choose. We only have to supply the will to do so. No other country in history has had this ability. The ruling classes of other great powers, the so-called elites or the political class, have robbed Peter to pay Paul since the beginning of time. While this means they can always count on the support of Paul, countries decline when Peter runs out of money.

In a masterful book, *This Time Is Different: Eight Centuries of Financial Folly*, authors Carmen Reinhart and Kenneth Rogoff present compelling evidence that we are close to the precipice.[45] When debt held by the public gets over 90 percent of GDP, countries find it hard to grow, leading ultimately to decline. (Note: There are two debt figures. The total debt, which is 100 percent of GDP, is less important because it includes debt of the federal government held by other federal entities.) Presently, our public debt is north of 70 percent and, based on projections, is headed toward 80 percent of GDP.

All we have to do is look at Greece. When a household overconsumes relative to what it produces, there are two ways out—consume less or produce more. Obviously, producing more is the best option. That is the growth option. Given our debt level, there is a window of time to pursue the growth option, but that window is closing. Everything else is austerity. This is what is happening with wages in Greece, as we can see in Figure 11-1.

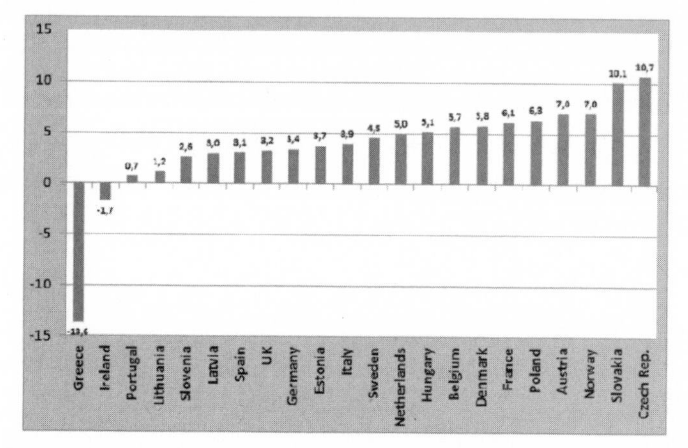

Figure11-1. Average hourly wage cost, showing percent change between 2009 and 2011. Note the figures for Greece. http://rwer.wordpress.com/2012/03/15/the-136-decrease-in-hourly-wage-costs-in-greece-after-the-third-quarter-of-2009/

Estimates vary on how long before we become Greece, but we must commit to never finding out. We may only have this election to make the right decision. How much longer can our economy tolerate this?

This is not a roller-coaster ride.

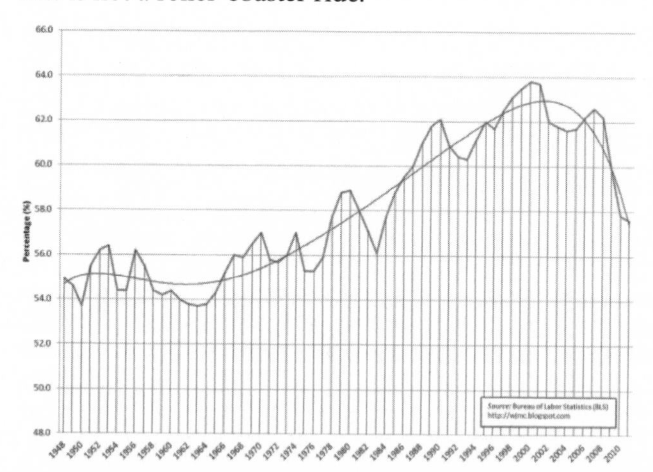

Figure11-2. U.S. employment-to-population ratio, 1948–2010. (Bureau of Labor Statistics, http://www.wjmc.blogspot.com.) http://rwer.wordpress.com/2011/02/23/graph-of-the-week-us-employment-to-population-ratio-1948-2011/#comment-14204

Figure 11-2 shows the percentage of the population that is working. This is the real unemployment rate. The unemployment rate the media prefer to report simply excludes those who have become so discouraged they quit looking for work. It makes the job market look better than it really is, but what do you expect of the media? They think we're stupid.

What makes this more startling is that fewer people working means fewer people are supporting the larger number of people who have dropped out of the labor force. This is not sustainable! When the employment ratio was lower during the 1948–1970 period, at least we had a low and stable price level so a family could make it on a single income.

And here is what big government's answer is to everything: print more money. Just like at the lemonade stand, debasing the currency only leads to higher prices. Figure 11-3 shows that the Fed has indeed substantially increased the money supply.

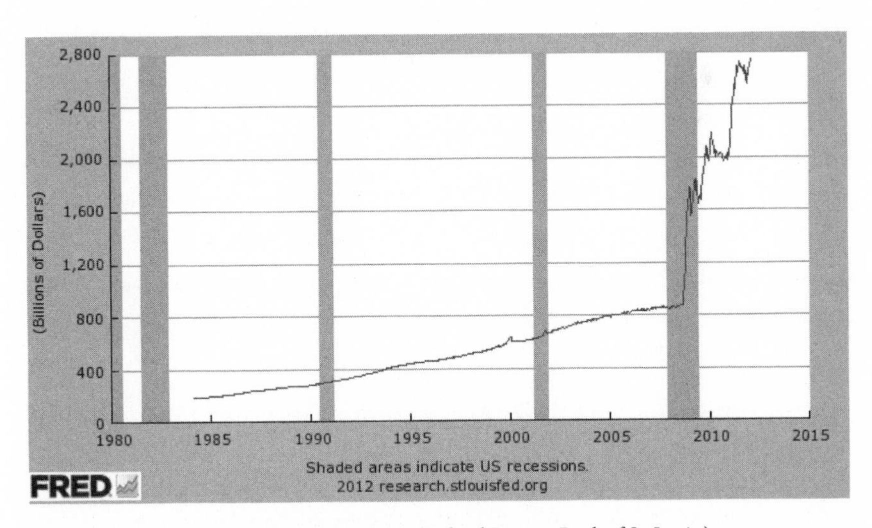

Figure 11-3. St. Louis adjusted monetary base. (Federal Reserve Bank of St. Louis.)

The Fed must be contained, or else it will try to print its way out of this, which only means a hidden tax, a confiscation of your income and your life savings, all at the hands of unelected bureaucrats.

Figure 11-4 shows the wage gap.

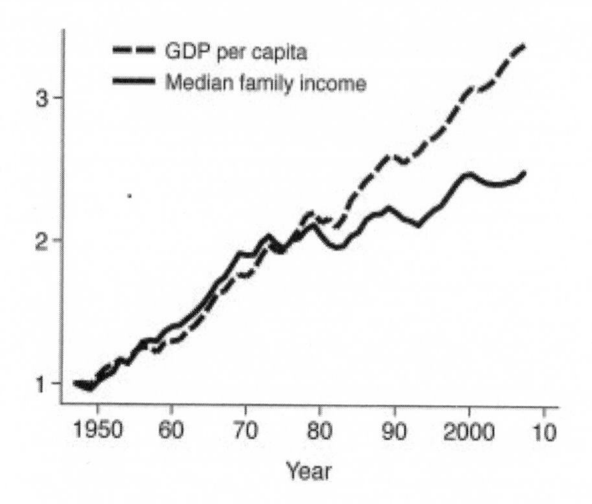

Figure 11-4. The decoupling of economic growth and middle-class income growth. (Lane Kenworthy, "Is Decoupling Real?" Consider the Evidence, March 11, 2012, http://lanekenworthy.net.)

To remove the gap, we must "tear down the wall" and transfer power back to the people, letting entrepreneurs and investors create solutions. If the current system worked, this gap wouldn't persist. It is the sign above all else that the system is broken and must be overhauled. Fortunately, our founders gave us everything we need to complete the job. We just have to join together.

This quotation from the great economist Ludwig von Mises captures the spirit of this book:

> *Used to the conditions of a capitalistic environment, the average American takes it for granted that every year business makes something new and better accessible to him. Looking backward upon the years of his own life, he realizes that many implements that were totally unknown in the days of his youth and many others which at that time could be enjoyed only by a small minority are*

now standard equipment of almost every household. He is fully confident that this trend will prevail also in the future. He simply calls it the American way of life and does not give serious thought to the question of what made this continuous improvement in the supply of material goods possible.[46]

The "American way" that makes for the continuous improvement in prosperity is liberty and free enterprise. With them as our guiding principles, the natural state of our economy is prosperity, and our Constitution guarantees that. We must take power back!

Join the Army of Davids. If we are informed, involved, and inspired, the big government Goliath of Washington, D.C., cannot defeat us.

The Solutions Revolution

Edmund Burke once said, "All that is necessary for the triumph of evil is that good men do nothing." I say, I will not die doing nothing. Join the Army of Davids against the big government Goliath. Visit the Cain Foundation website at www.cainfoundations.com.

And here is a poem for us to end on:

The Solutions Revolution

Socialism is rejected overtly,

So progressives pursue it covertly,

By having government construct a WALL,

That only obstructs the small.

They cut a deal with big corporations,

"If you accept tons of new regulations,

We will hand you on a silver platter

A cost-of-capital advantage that matters."

We'll dish you loopholes throughout your tax code

Making small business shoulder the real load.

Under the strain of expensive compliance,

Small business gets fed to the giants.

The Fed's boom-bust cycles put icing on the cake,

Feeding them sweet tidings of companies crushed in the wake.

As the Bigs eat all the competition,

They don't realize their own volition

Puts us on a road we did not choose,

Now our liberty we may soon lose.

Since those Bigs are so politically correct,

They were unwilling to stand up and reject

A deal crafted for them by the devil.

Now freedom holds the weight of that anvil!

We're pinned hard under Goliath's giant thumb,

And he must think that we're so dumb.

But let's now end his elitist dreams

He can't turn a deaf ear to our screams.

We the People have the Solution:

Take back power with a new Revolution.

An Army of Davids led by Herman Cain

Will join forces to slay Goliath again!

Things will be prosperous once and for all,

When we finally decide to TEAR DOWN THAT WALL!

To join a revolution without a bullet or bomb

Go to CAINFOUNDATION.COM.

Notes:

Chapter 1: Tinkering Won't Work

1. Arthur Laffer, Donna Arduin, and Wayne Winegarden, *The Prognosis for National Health Insurance*, a report prepared for the Texas Public Policy Foundation, August 2009, http://www.laffercenter.com/wp-content/uploads/2011/04/2009-08-RR04-HealthCare-Laffer-final.pdf.

2. Brian Domitrovic, *Econoclasts: The Rebels Who Sparked the Supply-Side Revolution and Restored American Prosperity* (Wilmington, Del.: Intercollegiate Studies Institute, 2009).

Chapter 2: The Right Diagnosis Yields the Right Cure

3. Internal Revenue Service, *National Taxpayer Advocate: 2008 Annual Report to Congress*, vol. 1, p. vi, December 31, 2008, http://www.irs.gov/advocate/article/0,,id=202276,00.html.

4. Arthur Laffer, *The Economic Burden Caused by Tax Code Complexity, Laffer Center for Supply-Side Economics,* April 14, 2011, http://www.laffercenter.com/2011/04/the-economic-burden-caused-by-tax-code-complexity/.

Chapter 3: The Right Way to Cut Taxes

5. Stanley Lebergott, *Pursuing Happiness: American Consumers in the Twentieth Century* (Princeton, N.J.: Princeton University Press, 1993).

6. The stock market tended to follow the ups and downs of tariff deliberations. The final committee hearings on October 28, 1929, indicated passage of the act. The stock market dropped the next day, on October 29; see Jude Wanniski, *The Way the World Works* (Washington, D.C.: Gateway Editions, 1998).

7. Arthur Laffer, "The Laffer Curve: Past, Present, and Future," Heritage Foundation Backgrounder, no. 1765, June 1, 2004. For revenue estimates, see Joseph A. Pechman, "Evaluation of Recent Tax Legislation: Individual Income Tax Provisions of the Revenue Act of 1964," *Journal of Finance* 20, no. 2 (May 1965). Actual revenues are from IRS, Statistics of Income, 1965.

8. Martin Feldstein, "What the '93 Tax Increase Really Did," *Wall Street Journal*, October 26, 1995.

9. Martin Feldstein and Daniel Feenberg, "The Effect of Increased Tax Rates on Taxable Income and Economic Efficiency: A Preliminary Analysis of the 1993 Tax Rate Increases," in *Tax Policy and the Economy*, vol. 10, ed. James M. Poterba (Cambridge, Mass.: MIT Press, 1996), pp. 89–118.

10. Austan Goolsbee, "What Happens When You Tax the Rich? Evidence from Executive Compensation," February 1999.

11. Ibid.

12. Arthur B. Laffer, Stephen Moore, and Jonathan Williams, "ALEC-Laffer State Economic Competitiveness Index," in *Rich States, Poor States*, 4th ed. (Washington, D.C.: American Legislative Exchange Council, 2011).

Chapter 4: The 9-9-9 Plan: Tax Code Replacement

13. Wanniski, *The Way the World Works.*

Chapter 5: The Benefits of 9-9-9

14. http://cainsolutionsrevolution.com/docs/999-National-Survey-Report.pdf.

15. Edward D. Kleinbard, "Herman Cain's 9-9-9 Tax Plan," Tax Notes, October 24, 2011, USC CLEO Research Paper No. C11–17, USC Law Legal Studies Paper No. 11–24.

Chapter 6: Regulatory Reform and the Creation of a Regulatory Budget Office

16. Nicole V. Crain and W. Mark Crain, "The Impact of Regulatory Costs on Small Firms," Small Business Research Summary 371 (September 2010), http://archive.sba.gov/advo/research/rs371tot.pdf.

17. James Gattuso and Diane Katz, "Red Tape Rising: Obama-Era Regulation at the Three-Year Mark," Heritage Foundation Backgrounder, March 13, 2012, http://www.heritage.org/research/reports/2012/03/red-tape-rising-obama-era-regulation-at-the-three-year-mark.

18. Business Roundtable et al. v. Securities and Exchange Commission (No. 10-1305, July 22, 2011), http://www.cadc.uscourts.gov/internet/opinions.nsf/89BE4D084BA5EBDA852578D5004FBBBE/$file/10-1305-1320103.pdf.

19. Gattuso and Katz, "Red Tape Rising."

20. Ibid.

21. Ibid.

22. Ibid.

23. The Administrative Procedure Act (PL 79-404) requires, among other things, that agencies publish a notice of proposed rule making, receive public comments, and consider those comments.

24. Executive Order 13422 (2007) amends Executive Order 12866 (1993). EO 12866 defines the rule-making review

process of the Office of Information and Regulatory Affairs. It also requires that each agency undertake an assessment of the potential costs and benefits of any significant regulatory action (defined generally as an annual effect on the economy of $100 million or more). See also EO 13258.

25. Executive Order 13563 (2011) requires agencies to undertake a retrospective analysis of existing regulations and seek public input to improve rules that "may be outmoded, ineffective, insufficient, or excessively burdensome, and to modify, streamline, expand, or repeal them in accordance with what has been learned."

26. Office of Management and Budget Circular A-4 defines federal best practices for agency cost-benefit analysis.

27. The Regulatory Flexibility Act of 1980 (PL 96-354) requires agencies to consider the views of the Small Business Administration Office of Advocacy and to undertake a regulatory flexibility analysis (RFA) or provide a certification that the regulation will have no "significant impact" on small entities.

28. Small Business Regulatory Enforcement Fairness Act of 1996 (PL 104-121), among other things, allowed judicial review of the adequacy of the RFAs conducted under the Regulatory Flexibility Act and liberalized the ability of small businesses to collect attorneys fees under the Equal Access to Justice Act when litigating with the federal government.

29. The Paperwork Reduction Act of 1980 (PL 96-511) requires that agencies obtain a control number and approval from the OMB's Office of Information and Regulatory Affairs

for forms that will impose an information collection burden on the general public. Once obtained, approval must be renewed every three years.

Chapter 7: Monetary Reform: A Case for Sound Money

30. John Maynard Keynes, *The Economic Consequences of the Peace* (New York: Harcourt, Brace and Howe, 1920), p. 235.

31. The formula for determining the number of such "exchange ratios" is ½ n(n - 1), where n is the number of goods. For example, if we have 1,000 goods in the economy and no currency, we would need to keep track of 499,500 prices.

32. Brian Domitrovic, "The Secret Term in the Fed's Triple Mandate: A Critical History," Laffer Center for Supply-Side Economics, November 28, 2011, http://www.laffercenter.com/2011/11/secret-term-feds-triple-mandate/.

33. William Clinton, *Clinton Global Initiative*, 2010.

34. Ralph Benko, "October Surprise: Can Gold Be the Panama Canal Treaty of 2012?," Forbes, October 31, 2011, http://www.forbes.com/sites/ralphbenko/2011/10/31/october-surprise-can-gold-be-the-panama-canal-treaty-of-2012/.

Chapter 8: A 21st Century Gold Standard

35. The chapter title of the authors' monetary reform policy shares the name of a booklet coauthored by Chuck Kadlec and Ralph Benko and commissioned by the American

Principles Project. Mr. Kadlec also cochaired the authors' policy. The authors wish to acknowledge the important contributions to the monetary reform effort made by the American Principles Project and by Mr. Benko. Not coincidentally, Mr. Benko, Mr. Kadlec, and Brian Domitrovic, another cochair of the authors' reform policy, are also advisers to the Gold Standard Now, which is, without pun intended, the "gold standard" of monetary reform organizations. The authors encourage the reader to examine Chuck and Ralph's booklet, which can be downloaded at http://agoldenage.com/. The authors hope their efforts to promote a specific monetary reform policy encourage the reader also to visit the websites http://www.thegoldstandardnow.org/ and http://americanprinciplesproject.org/category/gold-standard. Finally, Mr. Kadlec, Mr. Domitrovic, and Herman Cain's adviser Louis Woodhill, along with Mr. Benko, publish regular columns in Forbes magazine. To receive alerts for their commentaries, sign up to follow them at forbes.com.

Chapter 9: Energy Independence and Security

36. Institute for Energy Research, http://www.instituteforenergyresearch.org/energy-overview/oil-shale/.

37. Institute for Energy Research, http://www.instituteforenergyresearch.org/2011/06/10/on-a-btu-basis-renewable-subsidies-are-49-times-greater-than-fossil-fuel-subsidies/.

Chapter 10: Peace Through Strength and Clarity

38. Paul Hoffmeister, "Monetary Policy and World War IV: Protecting the American Economy and Neutralizing Al Qaeda's Financial Advantage," 2009.

39. Louis Woodhill, "Worried About Ahmadinejad, Chavez, and Putin? Stabilize the Dollar," *Forbes*, September 28, 2011, http://www.forbes.com/sites/louiswoodhill/2011/09/28/worried-about-ahmadinejad-chavez-and-putin-stabilize-the-dollar/.

40. Hoffmeister, "Monetary Policy and World War IV."

41. Ibid.

42. Paul Hoffmeister to Rich Lowrie, e-mail, January 29, 2012.

43. Woodhill, "Worried About Ahmadinejad, Chavez, and Putin?"

44. Ibid.

Chapter 11: The Solutions Revolution

45. Carmen Reinhart and Kenneth Rogoff, *This Time Is Different: Eight Centuries of Financial Folly* (Princeton, N.J.: Princeton University Press, 2009).

46. Ludwig von Mises, *Economic Freedom and Interventionism* (Indianapolis: Liberty Fund, 2006), p. 7.

An Army of Davids